How the Racers Ski

HOW THE

RACERS SKI

by Warren Witherell

Drawings by Mary Kelly

W · W · NORTON & COMPANY, INC · NEW YORK

Library of Congress Cataloging in Publication Data

Witherell, Warren.
  How the racers ski.

   1. Skiis and skiing. I. Title.
GV854.W54   796.9′3   72–6054
ISBN 0–393–08429–9

PRINTED IN THE UNITED STATES OF AMERICA

2 3 4 5 6 7 8 9 0

To Karen—whose faith, humor, editing, and typing have made this book possible.

And to the racers who have been my teachers.

Contents

[7]

PART IV   SKI SCHOOL

PART V   EQUIPMENT

PART VI   ESPECIALLY FOR RACERS

PART VII   ESPECIALLY FOR COACHES

Introduction

The purpose of this book is twofold: to provide competitive skiers with a guide to modern racing technique; and to offer recreational skiers a more natural and efficient way to ski than is now taught in most ski schools. International-class racers are constantly developing more efficient ski techniques. They are striving for optimum balance, economy of motion, and use of their skis to create turning forces. This book focuses on these fundamentals.

part I
Your Skis

chapter 1

"How Do I Look, Coach?"

Whenever I coach a young racer with whom I have had no previous contact, I ride with him to the top of the lift and ask him to ski a few hundred yards, so I can observe his technique.

Imagine the position of a young skier making his first demonstration for the "head coach." Of course, he is nervous. But he's anxious to begin training, and to learn something new. So he starts down the mountain. What does he *think* about?

Almost every new student is self-conscious about his *body position*. He wonders if he's twisting and bending enough at the waist, if he's holding his hands properly, if his hips are in the right place. The self-conscious skier is wondering: "How do I look, coach?"

But I am not looking—at his shoulders, or his hips, or his hands. *I am looking at his skis*—at the tracks they are leaving in the snow. I am judging whether he *carves* turns or skids them. I am judging the precision and range of his *edge control*. I am evaluating his use of the *tools* on which he is skiing.

By watching a racer's skis, I can judge his ability to ski with speed and precision. If I observed the racer's body, I would learn only of his *input* to technique; by studying his skis, I learn the *result* of his technique.

This book will focus on what the ski is doing in* the snow—and on what the ski can be made to do by changes in pressure, and in angle of edging. Most pressure and edge changes should be instituted primarily by ankle and knee movement. Upper-body rotation and exaggerated unweighting are relatively unimportant factors in modern race technique. The accomplished racer has progressed beyond body-oriented turning methods. Racing technique is now *ski oriented*. (See Drawing 1.)

[13]

(Drawing #1)

SKI IN SOFT SNOW

SKI IN HARD SNOW

* Most skiers are accustomed to speaking of the ski on the snow. The ski edge, in fact, cuts into the snow surface during all carved turns. To be technically accurate, we must think of the ski in the snow.

chapter 2

The Ski
Is a Tool

Snow skis are not 2 by 4's. They are carefully designed tools with controlled camber, flex, side-cut, torsion, etc. The most advanced skis have been developed through racer-oriented testing programs. The skis have thus been engineered to respond precisely to the techniques outlined in this book. Stated simply—the skis are designed to carve an arcing path through the snow when they are sufficiently rolled on edge, and when sufficient pressure is applied to bend them into reverse camber. (See Photo 1.)

The most basic concept in modern racing technique is this:
IF YOU STAND CORRECTLY ON YOUR SKIS, THEY WILL TURN FOR YOU. IF YOU APPLY CORRECT EDGE ANGLE AND PRESSURE TO A SKI, THE SKI IT-SELF WILL PROVIDE MOST OF THE REQUIRED TURNING FORCES.

If you wish to ski as the best racers do, you must learn to *carve* turns—i.e., turn without skidding or sideslipping. When a racer turns, he "feels" the texture of the snow and the shape of the terrain; he is sensitive to the flex and shape of his skis; he applies correct edge angle and pressure to his skis in the snow—and then he stands loose and flows with them. His upper-body movements are completely natural and relaxed. His body is free to maintain balance in response to terrain.

By contrast, most recreational skiers, including many instructors, constantly assume forced and self-conscious body positions. They try to change the direction of their skis through upper-body movements (rotation, counter-rotation, split-rotation, etc.)—and after achieving a desired line, they worry anew about a "proper" stance for each following traverse. They are concerned with final forms rather than fluid motion. To verify this observation, watch the public carefully next time you ride a chairlift. Or watch a group of ski instructors at a certification exam. Or watch instructor and class during a ski lesson. They're incredibly self-conscious and constrained.

1. *Becky Dorsey, 15-year-old winner of the 1972 Pabst Cup Can-Am Giant Slalom, carves an arcing turn. Note: (1) her ski is rolled on edge so the plane of the ski base is 45 degrees from the plane of the snow; and (2) her weight (increased by centrifugal force) has bent the downhill ski into reverse camber. The arc of Becky's turn is equal to the arc of her bent ski. Rather than skidding across the snow, she is carving a track through it—always letting her ski slide forward. This sliding of the ski with minimal resistance from the snow is called* glissement *by the French. It is the ultimate goal of racing technique.*

Many ski technicians argue that all turns must be started with some upper-body movement. In a sense they may be right. Certainly racers lean to initiate turns—but they do so as naturally as a child leans to turn a bicycle. Racers don't think about body movement. How you *think* about skiing is important. Most skiers *think* their upper bodies control each turn—so their body motions are self-conscious. Racers *think* their skis control each turn—so their body motions are more natural. A racer may move his body to change edge or pressure on his skis, or to anticipate changes in balance, but he does not think about moving his body. He thinks about the different feel of his ski edges in the snow, or about the line in the snow he wants his skis to follow.

The superior balance that racers exhibit results from their lack of self-consciousness about body positions. Most recreational skiers are frequently out of balance because they assume particular body positions learned from ski schools or ski magazines. These defined positions restrict a skier's natural reaction to terrain changes. Whenever the upper body is consciously used to create rotational forces, it is restricted from seeking natural balance. As balance adjustments are particularly required during periods of edge and direction change, it is desirable to provide maximum freedom to the upper body at these times. By disengaging the upper body from an active role in creating turning forces, a racer frees his hands, arms, and torso to make relaxed, natural balance adjustments in response to terrain variations.

Photo 1

IT IS NOT POSSIBLE TO SKI LIKE A RACER UNTIL YOU ARE COMPLETELY CONVINCED THAT CONSCIOUS UPPER-BODY MOTIONS ARE AS UNNECESSARY IN SKI TECHNIQUE AS IN WALKING. Most traditional ski technicians will choke over this idea. It is, however, a central idea to the thesis of this book. Let's pursue the argument.

Consider running down a dry stream bed—one consisting of variously shaped boulders and rocks. Think for a moment how difficult this activity is. The boulders are unevenly spaced. Some are round, some pointed. A few have flat tops, but most are tilted. Each requires a different angle of attack and departure. This physical activity is extremely complex. How do you progress down the stream? Do you consciously angulate? Do you think about unweighting or leading with your outside arm? Do you employ reverse shoulder because Stein Erikson does? Of course not. You just run. Your body balances quite naturally, though each step is a different length, and each landing place on a different angle.

What do you *think* about when running in a stream bed? *You think about your feet*—specifically about placing your left foot on a green rock, then your right foot on a gray rock. You pick a point with your eyes, and your foot goes to it. As your foot moves to a rock, every other part of your body follows in perfect balance. If you must land on a slippery rock, you feel the rock with the soles of your feet or sneakers —just as racers feel the snow. You use the nerves in your feet and the muscle tension in your legs to sense whether you will grip on the rock or slide off. If you feel you are sliding, you "edge" more. You edge by rolling your ankle and knee "into the hill." To balance that lateral movement, your upper body instinctively tilts (angulates) away from the hill. Throughout this exercise, you think mostly about the surface on which you are standing, or about the next point on which you will land. When skiing, a good racer picks a spot on the snow with his eyes, and his skis go instinctively to it. His body follows as naturally as your body follows your foot to a green rock.

What this comparison shows is that *body motions* are no more difficult in skiing than in streambed-running. In fact, balance is simpler when skiing—almost constant contact can be maintained with the snow, (as opposed to being airborne between rocks); and a skier can often stand on two feet simultaneously (while a runner is limited to one foot at a time). What makes skiing difficult for most people is that they cannot direct their feet as easily with skis attached as with sneakers attached. The goal of this book is to teach you the art of directing your skis as easily as you direct your feet. When you learn this art, skiing becomes as natural as walking. Follow me.

chapter 3

The Design of Modern Skis

It is impossible to discuss modern racing technique without first understanding the basic qualities of the tool that is being used—the ski, attached to your foot, ankle, and lower leg by a stiff boot. Racing technique depends on utilization of ski design as the primary factor in most turns. The fundamental design characteristics of modern skis are:

Camber describes the arched shape of a ski as it lies unweighted on a flat surface.

(Drawing #2)

THE FUNCTION OF CAMBER: Camber distributes the weight of a skier along the entire running surface of a ski. If a ski were built flat (without camber) most of a skier's weight would be carried by the mid-portion of the ski. On flat terrain the tip and tail would carry little of a skier's weight. Camber causes some of a skier's weight to be borne by the tip and the tail of his ski. This is the classic explanation of camber.

Racers think of camber in another way. When they stand in the middle of their skis, camber causes the tips and the tails to press into the snow. For a graphic demonstration of this point, place a ski on a flat table. With your index finger under the widest part of the tip, have someone press down on the center of the ski. Your finger will be pressed against the table. When you stand on skis in a neutral position, camber causes the tips and the tails to have pressure contact with the snow. This pressure is required to initiate all carved turns, and to maintain sufficient pressure toward the tips and tails of the skis to prevent skidding during sustained turns.

Reverse Camber describes the arc of a ski that is bent more than flat.

Because of its shape, when a ski is on edge, the tip and tail hold up the ends while a skier's weight depresses the center. (See Drawing 3.)

(Drawing #3)

The graceful arc of a ski edge—when the ski is bent into reverse camber—determines the arc of a carved turn. All carved turns require reverse camber in the ski.

Flexion describes the resistance of a ski to bending.

Commonly called "stiffness," flexion varies at different points along the ski. Most modern skis are stiffer in the tail than in the tip. The variation of flexion determines the flex pattern of a ski—that is, the arc it assumes in reverse camber.

Side-cut describes the shape of a ski edge as compared to a straight line. Side-cut can be varied in almost infinite ways. It is determined by the varying width of a ski from tip to tail. Although it is difficult to express in a formula, side-cut is the simplest factor in ski design to copy; it can be traced. It does not depend (as do camber, torsion, and flexion) on the material properties of a ski.

THE FUNCTION OF SIDE-CUT: As a ski is rolled on edge, side-cut causes the tip and the tail to carve into the snow. To visualize this, place a ski on a flat table and turn it on edge—first 10 degrees, then 20, 40, and 60 degrees. As you increase the edge angle, the tip and tail develop greater "bite" on the table—and the center of the ski can be further depressed until the ski develops reverse camber. This is exactly what happens when a racer makes a carved turn. (See Photo 2.)

Torsion describes the resistance of a ski to twisting. Torsion is usually measured with the center of the ski in a fixed position so that tip and tail torsion can be measured separately. Torsion can be measured at any point of the ski. A primary reason fiberglass skis are superior to wood and metal is that torsion can be more easily varied at any point along the ski by variations in glass application—by the amount, direction, and tension of the glass fiber patterns.

THE FUNCTION OF TORSION: To appreciate the function of torsion, place a ski once more on a flat table. Holding the middle of the ski, roll it 45 degrees on edge. Note that the tip and tail of the ski rock on edge too. If the ski had no torsional strength, the tip and tail would continue to lie flat on the table. Imagine skiing on a ski with too little torsional strength. Whenever you edged such a ski, the tip and tail would remain flat on the snow. The ability of the ski to carve a turn would be greatly diminished.

If a ski has too much torsional strength in the tip it will "hook" excessively when edged. When a ski is carving a turn, the tip must twist and untwist as it contacts varying terrain. Some torsional flexibility works as a shock absorber, helping the tip to follow undulations in the snow. Excessive torsion in the tail of a ski will cause it to track, making it difficult to initiate or sustain turns. Achieving a proper balance of torsion and side-cut is much like finding the ideal spring stiffness for an automobile suspension. Ski racers, like auto racers, require a stiffer suspension than do Sunday tourists.

COMBINING THE FUNDAMENTALS OF SKI DESIGN

A proper combination of camber, flexion, side-cut, and torsion causes a ski to carve a precise path through the snow. *In properly carved turns the entire edge of a ski passes through the same groove in the snow.* The tip of the ski leads the turn, and the remainder of the ski edge follows in the same track. (See Photos 2A, B, C, D, E, F.)

Camber, side-cut, and torsion are the principal factors in ski design which cause a ski to turn. There are numerous other factors which contribute to the excellence of a ski's performance—creating subtle differences in ski behavior not only between different brands of skis, but between different pairs of the same make and model. Briefly, these other characteristics are:

1. *Camber recovery:* The capacity of a ski to recover from a flexed position.

2. *Unwinding:* The capacity of a ski to recover from a twisted (torsionally deflected) position.

3. *Vibration:* The rapid fluttering of a ski tip—especially at high speeds on hard snow.

4. *Damping:* The quality of a ski to absorb vibration and other shocks.

5. *Side-deflection:* The capacity of a ski to be flexed sideways.

A

B

MALCOLM REISS

2A, B, C, D. In this photo sequence, Becky Dorsey is shown practicing downhill turns from a high tuck position. Her speed is about 40 MPH. Becky carries nearly all of her weight on her downhill (or outside) ski. She uses her inside ski only for balance in the first two photos. In the last two photos, she has picked up her left ski to step into the following turn.

No appreciable rotation or even steering is used in this turn. Becky simply rolls her right ski on edge, and applies sufficient pressure to the ski to create the reverse camber required to carve the turn. Centrifugal force increases her effective body weight on the ski. This turn perfectly illustrates the concept that "if you stand on your ski properly, the ski itself will provide the turning forces you desire."

Becky surprised the ski world last winter by winning the first Can-Am race from the last starting position. It was her first major race. A week later she finished second in the Madonna Cup Can-Am Downhill. Her secret?— the ability shown here to carve turns with minimum skidding.

C

D

Photo
2E

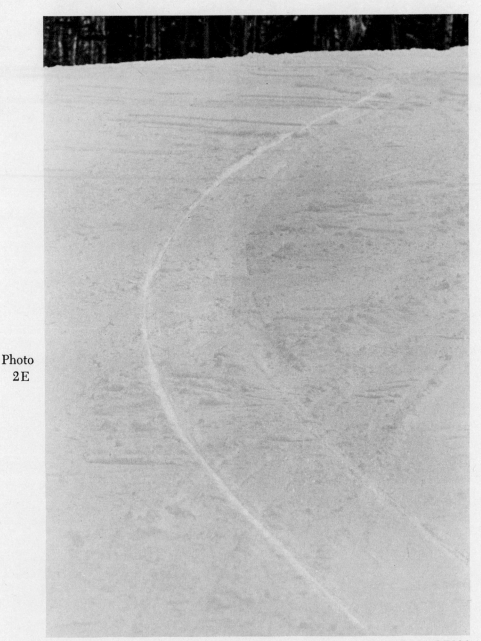

MALCOLM REISS

2E. This photo shows the track left by Becky's skis in the above turn. The weight distribution on the outside ski is clearly evident. The entire ski edge has passed through the same groove in the snow. In a turn of this kind, the ski runs with incredible smoothness. Because there is no sideslip, there is no chatter or instability. If you can imagine riding your own skis around a groove as neat as this one, you will begin to sense the joy of making pure carved turns.

Photo
2 F

2F. *In this photo, my pole points to the most pronounced bank made by Becky's ski. The angle of bank shows how much her ski was on edge. This part of the track corresponds to the second picture in the sequence above. Notice the angle of Becky's lower leg to the snow. The lateral displacement of her knee provides the edge angle required for this perfectly carved turn.*

This is measurable in inches or mms of deflection obtainable under a given amount of pressure (½ inch per 100 pounds etc.). This characteristic of modern ski design and construction is closely interrelated with side-cut, torsion, and camber. The results of variable side-deflection are not yet thoroughly understood, as design control of this factor is relatively new. Skis with a solid wooden core have very little side deflection. Channel-construction fiberglass skis (such as Head X-R 1 and Rossignol GTA) and foam-core skis such as K2 have much greater side-deflection than solid-core skis. This contributes to a ski's ability to "snake" on the snow when on edge. This sometimes helps a ski hold on ice, but it obviously changes the camber–torsion–side-cut balance.

All of these characteristics are closely related to the materials used in ski manufacture. Fiberglass, for instance, is more "damp" than metal. Foam cores deflect more than plywood. The problems of combining these many factors into a properly balanced tool must be left to ski designers and manufacturers. Their job is sometimes scientific, and sometimes guesswork. It involves a great deal of trial and error. It is

3. James Quinn, a 12-year-old racer, executes a carved turn. Note how the tip and tail of his downhill ski bite into the snow. Side-cut, camber, and torsion all contribute to the action of the ski in the snow.

MALCOLM REISS

STOWE REPORTER

4. In this picture, U.S. Olympian Terry Palmer's ski tips have passed over a bump and lost contact with the snow. The tip of his left ski is, because of camber, seeking snow contact. We call this the "snaking" action of a ski. The back part of Palmer's ski, which is supporting his weight, is still bent into reverse camber. Palmer is entirely committed to a carving turn, as opposed to a skidding turn. His edges must hold or he will fall. His extreme inward lean is required to be in balance because of the centrifugal force generated in this turn. Studying this photo, try to imagine the path and actions of Palmer's skis as this turn began, and as it will end. The same techniques employed by Palmer to make this dynamic turn are useful for relaxed, efficient, recreational skiing.

important to appreciate the interrelatedness of each factor in ski design. One factor cannot be changed without altering the balance of many. **Photos 3,4**

Few skiers in the world can ski on a poor pair of skis and identify the exact design fault(s). But any good racer can tell instantly when he has an exceptional pair of skis on his feet. They perform! They react precisely and predictably to each input of the racer's technique. The problem before us is to learn how to use the sophisticated tools now available. (See Photos 3 and 4.)

chapter 4

The Results of Ski Design (What a Ski Will Do)

Modern skiing is a process of standing correctly on your skis—of applying to your skis varying edge angles and pressures to achieve a desired performance.

If you roll a ski on edge, and apply sufficient pressure to create reverse camber, the ski will turn. As you increase the amount of edge angle and/or pressure, the ski will turn more sharply. The sharper turn results from an increase in reverse camber. Once a turn is begun and the ski is carving, additional pressure is applied to the ski by centrifugal force—the skier's mass trying to drift outside in the turn while the carving edge provides resistance. (Study Photos 1 and 3. Imagine the function of centrifugal force and edge angle in each picture.)

The arc of a turn remains constant as long as the same pressures and edge angle are applied to the ski, and the terrain remains the same. Any change in edge angle, pressure, or terrain will change the turning radius of the ski.

Forward, neutral, or back *pressure distribution* on a ski influences the arc a ski carves in the snow.

Forward *pressure distribution* bends the front of a ski more than the back.

(Drawing #4A)

This helps to initiate turns, or to shorten the radius of a turn in progress.

Neutral *pressure distribution* bends a ski on an even arc.

(Drawing #4B)

This is ideal for sustained turns of a constant radius.

Back *pressure distribution* bends the back of a ski more than the front.

(Drawing #4C)

This can be useful at the end of quick turns, or for turns of minimal direction change on relatively easy terrain.

A ski will stop turning when the edge assumes a straight line—i.e. when the reverse camber that sustains the turn is neutralized. I call this "neutralizing a ski," or "neutralizing a turn." For any given traverse, there is a combination of edge angle, pressure, and pressure distribution which causes a ski edge to carve a straight path.

It is always a delicate balance between changes of edge angle, pressure, and pressure distribution that neutralizes the turning power of a ski. The exact movements required to *neutralize* a ski vary with every turn. They depend on the terrain, snow condition, speed, type and condition of ski—almost infinitely changing variables. Only by experimentation can a skier learn the *many* ways a turn can be neutralized. It is a fine art—one mastered by experience and experiment. A skier's "feel" for the snow is especially important at this point where turns end and traverses begin.

It is difficult to picture the carving action of a ski simply by reading about it. You must *feel* it. Go out on the snow and experiment. The simplest carving action of a ski can be experienced on relatively flat terrain and at medium speed by spreading your skis about two feet apart, still parallel, and putting most of your weight on one ski—let's use the right. (Carry some weight on your left or inside ski to maintain balance and directional control). Roll your right ski 30 to 45 degrees on edge by moving your knee to the inside. If you just stand on your ski—with enough pressure to bend it into reverse camber—your ski will carve a long arc in the snow. Don't push the tail out or thrust the ski laterally in any way. Make long, gradual turns left and right close to the fall line by shifting your weight alternately from one ski to the other. Keep both skis parallel but two feet apart throughout this exercise. Your inside ski, which is lightly weighted and just providing balance, should drift easily as the downhill ski carves each turn. (See Photos 5A and B.)

5A. Cathy Bruce, a gifted young skier in the Burke Mountain Progam, practices wide-stance parallel turns. Concentrating on one leg at a time (here it is her right), Cathy explores the reaction of her skis to various amounts of edge angle, pressure, and leverage. Though she appears to be standing mostly on her left foot, centrifugal force places more than half her weight on the right ski.

MALCOLM REISS

Photos
5A;5B

5B. The photo above shows the long, carving tracks left by Cathy.
The arrow points to that phase of the turn that corresponds to the picture
opposite. Note the similarity between Cathy's turn and the high-speed racing
turn made by Becky Dorsey in Photo 2.

6. The French racer Bernard Orcel approaches a giant slalom gate. His inward lean anticipates the sharp turn he is about to make. His right ski carries most of his weight, and is edged more than 50 degrees. In the next moment, Orcel will apply forward pressure to the edged ski; this pressure will initiate the carved turn. Note Orcel's erect and square stance. This stance offers maximum balance and strength to a racer.

To vary the radius of your turns, experiment with different edge angles and pressure applications. Vary forward and back pressure distribution. Explore the reactions you can get from a nonskidding, edged ski. You will note that a little forward pressure helps initiate a sharper turn. Most carved turns begin with forward pressure distribution and are characterized by a forward push of the feet in the middle of the turn. Experiment with this pushing ahead of your feet to bring your skis to a position of neutral pressure distribution. Turns can be ended by reducing pressure at this point.

Obviously this kind of turn is of too long a radius to be useful on steeper terrain, but it is a *pure carved turn*. It will help you to feel your ski turn without skidding. Study the track you leave in the snow. There should be a definite line left by the edge of your ski. If there is enough loose snow, the groove of your ski will leave a raised track as well.

This wide-stance, pure-carve exercise is useful for teaching carved turns even to very accomplished racers. It helps them learn to initiate turns with no lateral push to edge or change the direction of their skis. To make a properly carved turn, a ski must be edged first, then have pressure and leverage applied to initiate its change of direction.

If you try to change the direction of a ski while it is still flat on the snow, some lateral skidding of the ski will occur. To prevent skidding, the carving edge must be in the snow before direction change occurs. Remember: *To make a pure carved turn—you must edge your ski first, then apply pressure and let it turn.* (See Photo 6.)

Photo
6

chapter 5

Controlling the Ski

There are four basic inputs to control a snow ski: EDGE—the angle of a ski base to the snow. PRESSURE—the amount of weight or downward force applied to a ski. LEVERAGE—forward, neutral, or aft application of pressure to a ski. TWIST—the rotational forces applied to a ski. These four elements can most precisely and quickly be varied by ankle and knee movement.

EDGE

The amount your ski is rolled on edge is an essential factor in each turn. As the degree of edging is increased, the ski:
1. Becomes more resistant to sideslip.
2. "Bites" increasingly at the tip and the tail.
3. Develops (because of side-cut) an increasing potential for reverse camber.

These three factors have a major effect on the sharpness of any turn.

Though slight changes in edge can be achieved by "rolling your ankle," this factor is limited in range by body structure, and by either the give in soft boots, or the immobilization of your ankle joint in stiff boots. Thus, while racers make very fine edge adjustments by ankle movements, LATERAL KNEE DISPLACEMENT IS THE PRIMARY METHOD OF ROLLING A SKI ON EDGE. Lateral knee displacement can be accomplished by 1) knee angulation; 2) hip angulation; 3) body lean; 4) any combination of these three. (See Drawing 5.)

I will refer often in the pages that follow to "edging a ski," "placing a ski on edge," or "increasing the angle of edge." Whatever phrase is used to describe this basic part of each turn, THE KNEES MUST ACCOMPLISH THE TASK BY MOVING LATERALLY IN RELATION TO THE SKIS. Lateral knee flexibility is a basic requirement of racing technique. The quickest way to change edge angle is by knee movement alone, as that requires a minimum displacement of body mass. Quick turns made close

(Drawing #5)

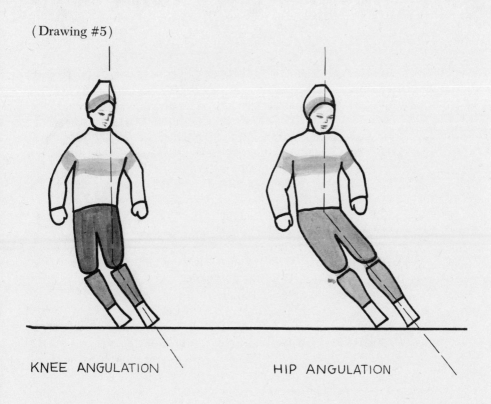

KNEE ANGULATION   HIP ANGULATION

INWARD LEAN   EXTREME ANGULATION

COMBINATION KNEE, HIP,
AND INWARD LEAN.

[35]

to the fall line require little more than knee angulation to edge the skis. Sustained turns across the fall line require more inward lean to maintain balance, and also greater edge angles to resist sideslip caused by centrifugal force. For such turns, hip angulation is required.

Angulation is both a natural movement of balance, and a method of edging your skis. Good skiers think primarily of the feel their skis have in the snow. They edge their skis by moving their *knees* and hips to the inside. Depending on the edge angles and inward lean required by any turn, their upper bodies adjust naturally to an angulated position. Don't think too much about angulation. Just edge your skis, relax, and let angulation occur naturally.

Photos 7A and 7B show two racers achieving an almost identical edge angle with quite different angulation. The photos are taken at the same gate in the 1972 Jr. National Giant Slalom.

How Much Edge Angle Do Racing Turns Require? In theory 45 degrees provides maximum resistance to sideslip on a very hard surface, but on normal snow (where the ski sinks into the surface) a greater degree of edge improves resistance. Even on very hard ice, edging beyond 45 degrees increases a ski's potential for reverse cam-

7A. *Leith Lende, the 1972 Junior National Combined Champion, exhibits a marked "break" at the hip joint. She combines knee and hip angulation to edge her skis; and she keeps her upper body almost vertical. This severe hip angulation is not possible from a square hip position, so Leith has turned her hips and shoulders. Leith's position is remarkably similar to that most commonly seen in pictures of Gustavo Thoeni at similar gates.*

MALCOLM REISS

MALCOLM REISS

7B. Sarah Pendleton, 1972 Corcoran Cup winner, exhibits a straighter upper-body lean combined with knee and hip angulation. This allows Sarah to maintain a more square hip position. There are advantages and disadvantages to both Sarah's and Leith's positions. (See Appendix.)

ber. How can you roll a ski on edge 40, 50, or 60 degrees? By combining knee and hip angulation with inward body lean.

Lateral deflection of your knees increases as you bend them. (See Drawing 6.)

Photos 7A, 7B

(Drawing #6)

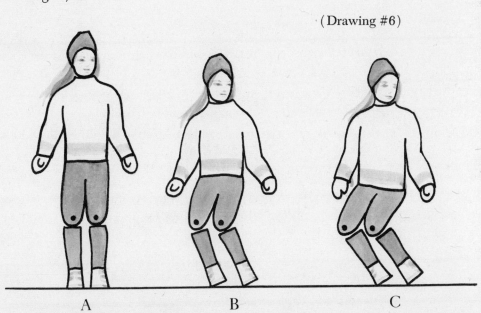

A   B   C

To appreciate this, stand on the floor with your legs straight and try to move your knees sideways. No lateral movement is possible. (See Figure A.) Now bend your knees 30 degrees and see how much they will move laterally. (See Figure B.) Now try at 60 degrees (Figure C). A 90-degree knee bend provides maximum lateral knee movement, but it is so low a hip position that you are left in too weak a stance on your skis.

Whenever severe edge angles are required, hip angulation and inward lean must be used. The average recreational skier will seldom need more than 10 to 20 degrees of inward lean. Good racers, however, especially in giant slalom, make very sharp turns at high speed. Inward lean as great as 60 degrees is often required.

"The Bicycle-lean Angle" In our coaching at Burke Mountain we call the amount of lean required to be in balance during a turn "the bicycle-lean angle." A more technical term is "inclination." If you want to turn sharply at high speeds, you must lean in to keep from falling to the outside of the turn. This inward lean contributes, of course, to the edge angle that makes sharp turns possible. A skier at 20 MPH turning in a one-hundred-foot radius requires a bicycle-lean angle of about 15 degrees. At 25 MPH and a twenty-foot radius the lean angle is about 53 degrees. As speed increases or radius decreases, a greater lean angle is required.

Whatever amount of inward lean is required for a turn, that lean serves both to balance your body and to edge your ski. You still must control the precise path your skis follow by subtle movements of your knees—laterally, forward, and backward.

PRESSURE

For all carved turns, sufficient pressure must be applied to a ski to bend it into reverse camber. The arc of reverse camber must be equal to the arc of the turn. The sharper the turn, the greater is the pressure required.

Pressure on a ski can be increased by:

1. Standing on one ski—which doubles the weight compared to a two-ski stance.
2. "Stomping" on one ski (or two)—quickly pushing down on a ski—as in stomping your foot on the ground.
3. Extending your hips or upper body, which exerts an equal and opposite downward force on your ski.

4. Tightening the radius of a carved turn so that increased centrifugal force increases the pressure of body weight applied to your ski.

Pressure is decreased on a ski by actions opposite to those above:

1. Moving weight from one ski to two.
2. Quickly picking your feet up.
3. Contracting your upper body.
4. Lengthening the radius of a turn.

LEVERAGE

"Leverage" and "pressure distribution" are almost synonymous—but not quite. Leverage defines the action of a skier—applying pressure forward, neutral, or aft. Pressure distribution defines the result of leverage—the distribution of pressure on various parts of the ski.

Leverage—forward, neutral, or aft—is most easily adjusted by ankle, knee, and hip movement. If your upper body is maintained in a neutral position, the forward–backward adjustment of your ankles, knees, or hips causes your lower leg to press on the front or back of your boot shaft. This pressure is transmitted to your ski. Ankle, knee, and hip movements also affect the percentage of weight applied to your skis through the ball or heel of your foot.

Good racers frequently adjust leverage (and pressure distribution) by sliding their skis forward or backward under their center of mass. Most racing turns are begun with a forward press of the knees, followed by a sliding ahead of the skis to bring them into a position of neutral or aft leverage. (See Drawing 7.)

(Drawing #7)

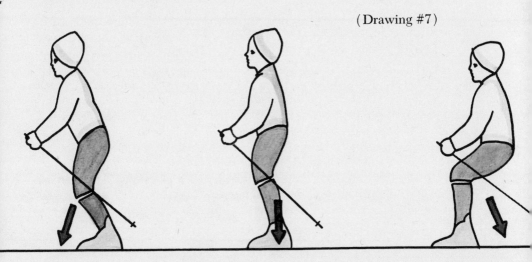

Whenever possible, leverage should be controlled by knee and ankle movement, as they are the lowest movable foundations in your stance. Excessive upper-body movements cause undesirable changes in balance with less efficient changes in leverage.

A ski, like an automobile, is most easily steered from the front. Most carved turns are initiated with forward leverage to increase control of the ski tip. As soon as the tip establishes the desired arc of a turn, pressure distribution should move to the center of the ski. If a quick acceleration turn is being made, pressure will flow rapidly from the tip—through the center—to the tail. The whole ski should be in contact with the snow whether forward, neutral, or back leverage is applied to make a turn. The difference is one of degree, and the result in ski performance is a question of where the maximum bend of the ski is placed.

Forward leverage places the most severe part of the reverse camber toward the tip. The front of the ski is bent more than the back. Review Drawings 4A, B, C, and D. If forward leverage is maintained throughout a turn, the tip (because it is bent more than the rest of the ski) acts as a brake and causes excessive chatter. Forward leverage should only be maintained while the radius of a turn is being shortened (i.e. while you are increasing the sharpness of a turn).

Neutral leverage flexes the ski on a nearly smooth arc. Sustained turns are best made with neutral leverage.

Back leverage moves the sharpest bend of the reverse camber toward the tail of the ski. Sustained sharp turns cannot be carved with back leverage because the side-cut is less severe in the back half of the ski than in the front half. Back leverage is best used for long-radius turns on relatively flat terrain; on steeper terrain, turns are often ended with back leverage to provide acceleration. A most important use of back leverage is to *complete with a carving action* all turns that are begun by *steering* a relatively flat ski.

TWIST

Not all turns can be purely carved. Turns of especially short radius and turns made at slow speeds often require the application of twisting forces to rapidly change the direction of a ski. For most turns, TWISTING FORCES SHOULD *supplement*, NOT REPLACE, THE CARVING ACTIONS OF A SKI.

Throughout this book I shall minimize discussion of twisting forces, because they are well understood already. Most existing ski techniques are based on twisting forces generated by upper-body movements and usually referred to as some kind of *rotation*. These movements have been analyzed so thoroughly in so many books that most skiers are overconscious of them. The movements, furthermore, are hardly ever required by modern ski technique. In most cases where twisting forces are required by a racer, he needs only to think about turning his feet, or occasionally his outside knee and leg. These forces are applied so instinctively they hardly require thinking about. Whenever you move your knee forward and inside to edge a ski, twisting force is automatically created. (Stand in wool socks on a smooth floor and move your right knee forward and in as to edge for a left turn: Your right heel will rotate outward.) This is a natural *steering* action.

WHEN RACERS USE TWIST, THEY APPLY IT IN CONJUNCTION WITH EDGE ANGLE AND PRESSURE. TWIST *assists* THE OTHER INPUTS TO CARVE A TURN. THIS COMBINATION OF FORCES I CALL *Steering*.

The primary uses of steering are:

1. To initiate turns at slow speed. When speed is insufficient to maintain the pressure and edge angle required for a carved turn, it is necessary to begin turns by steering the ski on the snow while the ski is relatively flat. The initial direction change of the ski is thus made by sideslipping—twisting the ski around its pivot point from a stance of nearly neutral leverage. These turns must be done with gentleness and a sensitivity for ski–snow friction so that minimum deceleration occurs. Direction change is initiated by steering, and the end of the turns should be carved.

2. When making any turn which is sharper than the arc of reverse camber that can be applied to a ski, some skidding must occur through a part of the turn. This skidding should involve the least possible sideways friction. If a 30-degree direction change is sought, the first 20 degrees may have to be steered on a relatively flat ski—then the final 10 degrees of turn made with a carving motion on a more edged ski. The proportions differ for every turn.

I believe that even a steered, flat ski turn should usually begin with subtle forward pressure—just enough to help initiate the turn of the ski. When the ski is slightly edged, a little forward leverage causes the edge to grab the snow just ahead of the pivot point. The design of the ski thus contributes some turning power.

All steering, as I use the term, involves some use of the ski to assist in turning it about its pivot point. *Steering is, therefore, more than twisting; it is a twisting of the foot or leg coordinated with as much use of ski design as is available for each circumstance.* Steering thus requires a particularly sensitive feel for the relationships between the ski edge and the snow. The sensitivity needed here is greater even than that required for a pure carved turn, because utilization of the ski design is so difficult at times when steering is required.

Steering, if properly done, adds the elements of a carved turn to all skidded turns. Even a skidded snowplow turn should not begin with heel thrust, but with steering that depends on subtle forward pressure and purchase of the inside edge just ahead of the center pivot point. After initiation, skidding must be done with neutral leverage.

Turns initiated by steering on a relatively flat ski must end on an edged ski to provide positive control and maximum speed in connecting traverses. (See Photos 8A and 8B.) The challenge to the expert skier is to end the skidding part of each turn at the earliest possible point. The transition from skidding to carving must be made with maximum pressure under the whole foot. Edge-set for each traverse must occur while the skier stands perfectly balanced with neutral leverage. Excessive leverage forward or back at the time of edge-set would cause the weighted end of the ski to grab, and the light end to slide downhill. After edge-set is achieved (i.e., the ski is carving) then leverage and pressure can move aft to complete the turn with a carving motion. If the turn is to be ended by carving, the edge-set and the initiation of back leverage should occur simultaneously. Thus the sharpest possible carving arc can be utilized.

The movements described here are tremendously subtle and can only be accomplished by a skier in perfect balance on his skis. Relaxed, disciplined, quiet upper-body positions are necessary to work so sensitively with the feet.

For high-speed carved turns, small steering forces are often required to start the direction change, and also to control subtle variations of arc during sustained turns. Most steering is best done from a wide stance, as it is easiest to twist your foot or lower leg when it is bearing weight well outside your hip. Steering is thus most natural from a wide stance, after a lateral step, or from an angulated position.

For a fuller understanding of the variety of ways a ski can be steered, I recommend study of George Joubert's *Teach Yourself to Ski.* Special attention should be given to his discussion of *"braquage,"* which he defines as "an inward push of the outside knee with a gradual pivoting effort of the same leg." This is the primary motion, according to Joubert, that initiates skidded turns and controls the arc of many carved turns.*

* George Joubert is Technical Director and Coach of the Grenoble University Ski Club. The author of seven books on skiing, he is generally considered the finest ski technician in the world today. *Teach Yourself to Ski* is available in English translation through Aspen Ski Masters, Aspen, Colorado. I recommend this book to all persons who are seriously interested in ski technique. Joubert has an enormous understanding of ski mechanics, and a rare ability to write clearly. In *Teach Yourself to Ski,* he covers a wide range of subjects not dealt with in this text. Also worthy of study is Joubert's 1966 publication, *How to Ski the New French Way.*

Photo
8A

8A. Burke Mountain coach Mike Raymaley demonstrates a steered turn. As the slope is gentle and his speed slow, Mike cannot make a pure carved turn. He edges his skis only moderately, and he uses their carving properties to control them in a narrow skid. His turn ends with a clean edge-set to provide maximum speed and stability in the traverse.

[43]

Photo
8B

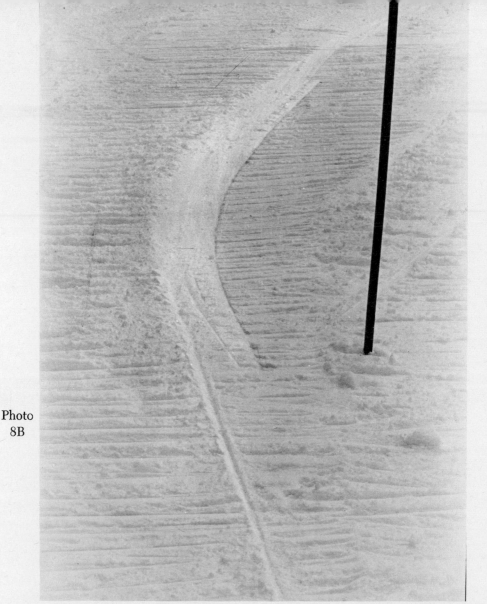

8B. *Here is the track Mike left in the snow. At the start of the turn, steering of the outside ski is evident while the inside ski is still carving. Both skis are skidding together in the middle of the turn. Though his outside ski bears most of his weight, Mike's inside ski maintains a light purchase on the snow throughout the turn. Mike uses the inside edge of the inside ski to help steer his turn. Both tracks show subtle combinations of carving and skidding techniques.*

At the earliest time Mike can end the skid on his outside ski, he does so. The ski leaves a definitive track where the turn ends and the traverse begins. In the instant he achieves the stability of this edge-set, Mike lifts his inside ski to step into the following turn. A less accomplished skier would leave a wider skidding track than Mike; and he would fail to achieve the definite traverse as early in the turn as Mike does.

In concluding this chapter, something must be said about *variety* in ski turns. No two turns are ever alike. One of the continually satisfying pleasures of skiing is the infinite variety of snow conditions and terrain that are offered to a skier. The principal fault of ski-school teachers and pupils is that they assume one formally defined style for too many turns where it's not suitable. Though I promote a simplified technique based on carving turns by edge angle and pressure variation, *I do not for a moment suggest that one technique serves all kinds of skiing.* Use of the ski by varying edge angle and pressure changes is the *theme* of modern race technique—*an infinite number of variations can be played on the theme.* You can carve turns whether forward or back, erect or hunched over—with your hands in your pockets or your ears, with your skis together or apart, with additional rotation or counter-rotation, on the uphill ski or the downhill ski or on both at once.

Hard ice, packed powder, or waist-deep fluff—all respond to variations of edge angle and pressure. A good racer can ski with precision and control on any snow surface. While most ski schools teach formal body movements that are repeated over and over again, the racer's movements have infinite variety, because every turn is a direct response to snow conditions and terrain.

chapter 6

The Carved Turn

T he preceding chapters on ski design and function assume use of a ski technique that stresses carved turns.

"Carved turn" does not define any particular body motion or body position. It describes only the *action of a ski.* In a pure carved turn there is no sideslip or skidding. The ski leaves a track in the snow equal to its width. In a skidded turn the ski leaves a much wider track, as the ski is turned at an angle to its direction of travel. (See Drawing 8.)

In the very best racing turns, the entire edge of the ski passes over the same spot in the snow. The tip initiates the turn, biting into the snow and setting a track or groove through which the remainder of the ski edge flows. The initiation of a carved turn is critically important. Once a ski begins to skid, its tendency is to continue skidding; if a carving action initiates a turn, it is easier to maintain the carving action at each succeeding point in the turn. Thus, the first direction change of the ski must occur without skidding. Heel thrust and rotation must be avoided.

To initiate a turn without skidding, *the ski must be edged before turning forces are applied.* Drawing 9 shows two ways to increase the edge angle of your skis.

Skier #1 maintains his knee and hip position while pushing his skis out. This lateral push begins a skidding turn. Undesirable braking and loss of balance result.

Skier #2 does not push sideways on his skis. He lets his skis run while moving his knees and hips. This angulating movement increases the edge angle of his skis without a skidding motion.

In summary—angulation and resultant increased edge angle can be achieved by pushing the feet out, or by leaning the body in. Carved turns require the latter movement.

It is important to state that the term "carved turn" is applied to turns where there is minimal skidding. It is extremely difficult to eliminate

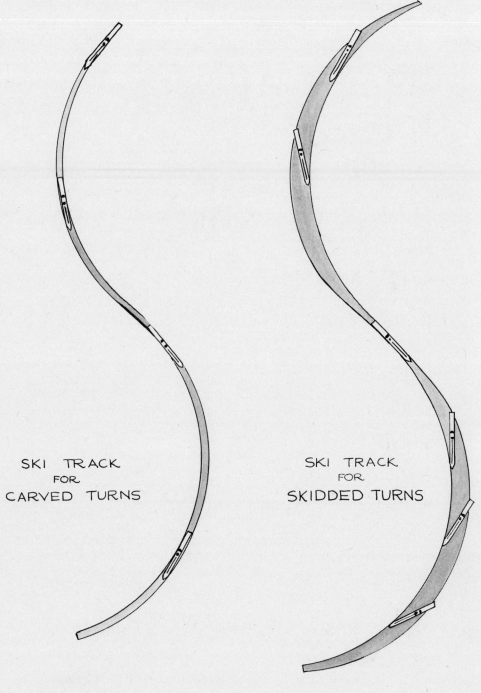

SKI TRACK
FOR
CARVED TURNS

SKI TRACK
FOR
SKIDDED TURNS

(Drawing #8)

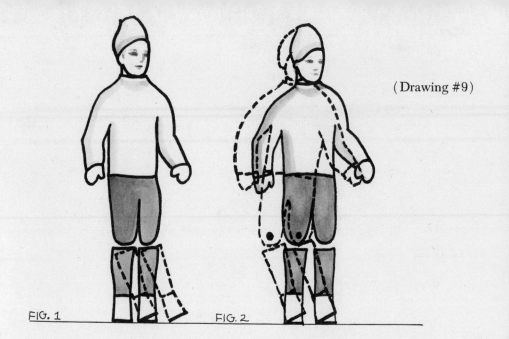

FIG. 1   FIG. 2

SIDEWAYS PUSH OF
FEET INITIATES
SKIDDING + BRAKING.

ANGULATION PROVIDES
INCREASED EDGE WHILE
SKI MAINTAINS CARVING PATH.

all skidding from all ski turns. Good racers skid very little. In common practice we call any turn a "carved turn" where the track of the ski is very narrow, and where the turn is made not by pushing the ski through a skid, but by applying edge angle and pressure as described in Chapters 4 and 5 and then relying on side-cut and reverse camber to dictate the path of the ski edge.

It is possible to make carved snowplow turns, stem turns, parallel turns, skating turns, etc. Any upper-body position can be assumed in a carved turn—so long as upper-body rotation is not used to twist the ski in such a way that it skids.

Carved turns require much less energy than skidded turns because no appreciable amount of body rotation, heel thrust, or unweighting is required to turn the ski. It follows that the total amount of body motion required for carved turns is significantly less than the motion required for skidded turns. This economy of motion is especially important in racing and in fast free-skiing.

Improved balance is an important factor favoring the use of carved turns. The elimination of excessive upper-body movements greatly reduces problems of balance which are normally encountered in rotation and skid techniques.

You can probably recall a time when you have lost your balance in a series of turns, then headed straight down the fall line until you regained your balance. The straight schuss, though it increased your speed, afforded a better opportunity to regain balance. Why should it be easier to regain balance while going straight, even though going straight requires going faster? The answer is clear: Balance is difficult in any skidding maneuver! Carved turns, by contrast, are made on a "tracking" or "running" ski; thus they require few balance adjustments.

Imagine a standard bicycle turn where the tires grip well on dry pavement. Balance is simple, requiring only a slight inward lean. But if the bicycle turn is made on wet grass or loose gravel which causes the bicycle to skid, then balance problems quickly increase. In a skidding turn, balance requirements are unpredictable and varied. In a carved turn, balance requirements are relatively predictable and constant. This explains why the best skiers can maintain quiet, well-balanced body positions even when making fast turns over difficult terrain.

It is important to remember that terrain often prohibits the contact of the entire ski edge with the snow. (See Photo 9.)

Photo
9

9. Billy Shaw (1972 Junior National Giant Slalom Champion) carves a turn with forward leverage, but there is no pressure at all on the tip of his ski. Only a few inches of Shaw's left ski is in the snow ahead of the ski's narrowest point, which is located a few inches behind the ball of his foot. Shaw's ski has effective side-cut in even those few inches. With most of the pressure applied near the center of the ski, Shaw still carves his turn, and forward leverage contributes to the carving action of his ski.

MALCOLM REISS

In all parts of this book where I talk of forward or back pressure on the ski, you must realize that the major weight distribution of the skier is seldom located far out on the tip or tail of the ski. The center section of a ski usually bears the majority of a skier's weight. Subtle changes in leverage distribute that weight sufficiently ahead or behind the waist of the ski to determine whether the turn is carved *relatively* on the front or back of the ski. We say a racer is "carving on the tip of his ski" when his balance point is only a few inches ahead of the waist of his ski. "Carving on the tip" does not require an extreme forward lean. Likewise, the back of the ski can be used from an almost neutral stance, and "carving on the tail" does not require use of an extreme sitting-back position. Modern racing skis are sensitive to very small adjustments of pressure distribution.

chapter 7

"But When Do I Skid?"

A racer should never skid a turn unless he is intentionally braking or stopping—or unless the turn is so sharp it cannot be made in a pure carving motion. Then *steering* is required. A recreational skier should skid turns only when he requires a braking action to control his speed. Such braking actions should be a last resort of speed control. Choice of terrain and line should determine speed whenever possible.

It makes no more sense to skid turns on skis than in automobiles. An automobile is most stable and most precisely controlled when the tires track without skidding. A skier has equally superior stability and directional control when his skis track without skidding. Likewise it is easier to stand on ice skates and go straight forward than to skid sideways. It is also easier on ice skates to make carved turns than skidding turns.

Everything written about ski design in Chapters 1 through 6 is based on use of the ski for *carved turns*. It is true that modern skis are designed so they will perform reasonably in skidding turns as well. But the most efficient use of the ski is in carved turns. *Despite this fact of ski design, and despite the obvious advantages of balance and efficiency, most ski schools continue to teach skidding turns to beginners —and also to base their advanced ski techniques on skidding turns.*

I BELIEVE THAT ANY SKI TECHNIQUE OR SKI TEACHING SYSTEM THAT IS BASED ON SKIDDING TURNS IMPOSES UNACCEPTABLE PROBLEMS OF BALANCE AND CONTROL ON THE SKIER. It is this difference that most widely separates racers from recreational skiers. If I had to reduce the content of this book to one sentence, I would say: "Racers carve turns rather than skid them." This entire book might be considered a treatise on "The elimination of skidding from snow-ski technique."

Skidding turns are braking turns. A skier who is perpetually skidding (whether turning or traversing) can ski close to the fall line without gaining excessive speed. A racer who carves turns—who lets his skis run without skidding—builds up speed very quickly unless he turns out of the fall line. Thus, on a hill of 20 degrees incline a racer would ski path A at 20 MPH; a skidder would ski path B at the same 20 MPH. (See Drawing 10.)

(Drawing #10)

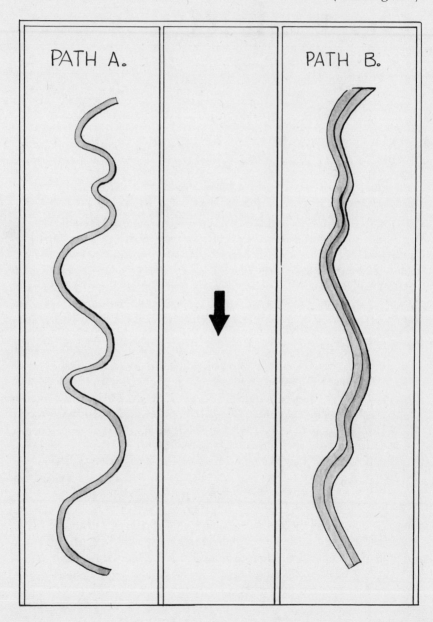

PATH A.   PATH B.

IF YOU CARVE TURNS—AND THUS MAINTAIN THE MAXIMUM SPEED POTENTIAL OF YOUR SKIS—YOU MUST TURN ACROSS THE HILL TO CONTROL YOUR SPEED. When you ski this way, two pleasures result: First, you have the joy of realizing maximum speed potential from your skis; and second, you develop an intimate relationship to the terrain as you use the hill to increase and decrease your speed. By contrast, the skidding skier is continually resisting, holding back, braking. He resists the speed of his skis and fights against the terrain on which he slides.

In coaching racers, I emphasize that when free-skiing they must never reduce speed by a skidding action of their skis. Every time they do this they reinforce muscular habits related to skidding turns. In every turn, a racer must strive for ultimate utilization of his ski to maintain and create speed. Only thus can he develop instinctive muscle habits related to the fastest possible technique. When a racer wants to go slower, he must turn out of the fall line, reducing his angle of descent by traversing across the hill. When free-skiing, racers must choose a slow line and try to go fast on it.

Skidded turns are taught in many ski schools precisely because they do create a braking action—and therefore provide speed control. I agree that recreational skiers should know how to skid in order to control speed, but this skid should be specifically applied only when braking is desired; it should not be the foundation of a turning technique. Control of speed by selection of line can be taught very early in ski-school programs and should be stressed for all intermediate to advanced skiers.

The elation that results when you feel your skis working for you—when you feel them responding to each precise change of edge and pressure—is one of the great thrills in snow skiing. This thrill is unknown to most skiers because they have been taught to use their skis as *brakes* rather than *accelerators*. To a racer, skis are accelerators; the terrain on which a racer skis offers a constant challenge to his ingenuity and skill in making his skis go faster on whatever line he chooses.

As a racer develops techniques that combine efficiency with good balance, he is able to ski a very fast line—and still to work constantly for more speed from his skis. This I believe is the greatest joy of skiing—and it is a joy that many recreational skiers have the ability to pursue.

How Is a Carved Turn Made?

Many coaches who have helped in the preparation of this book have suggested I present a step-by-step analysis of how a carved turn is made. I hesitate to define a single turn, for fear that people will take

10. The author free-skiing at a moderate recreational speed. His stance is relaxed, erect, comfortable. Note the minimum arm movement required to plant the left pole.

it as a new gospel, and will try to make all turns in exactly the same way. In truth, no two turns are exactly alike. Terrain, speed, and line are always changing. Still, there are common elements in most turns. The following generalizations may be helpful.

1. An unweighting motion—extension, contraction, step etc.—can be used to facilitate edge change, ending one turn and beginning another. But your skis should not normally come off the snow. Keep your skis tracking, and maintain a feel for the snow. Unweighting motions should be more subtle than for most skid-turn techniques; indeed, no unweighting is required for many carved turns. Only edge change is required. Edge change should be accomplished with as quiet and balanced a body position as possible. There should be *no* upper-body rotation to twist your skis at the moment of edge change.

2. Following edge change, roll your skis sufficiently on edge to prohibit sideslip and to create the required potential for reverse camber. DO NOT SKID YOUR SKIS LATERALLY TO INCREASE EDGE ANGLE. (See Drawing 9, page 48.) Let your skis "run," and use angulation to increase edge angle.

3. After your skis are sufficiently edged (though edge angle may still be increasing) apply pressure and forward leverage until reverse camber is achieved and your ski tip carves an arcing path through the snow.

4. Allow the tightening radius of your turn to increase pressure on your skis, creating more reverse camber. When the arc of your turn is established, adjust to neutral leverage to sustain your turn. Use also extension or contraction of your body, and adjustment of weight distribution on one or two skis to control pressure.

5. Relax. Stand loose. Stay square. Don't rotate. Don't lean into the turn with your head or shoulders. Keep your hands in front of you at equal elevation and equal spread. Keep your body quiet and let your skis create the turning forces. Stand mostly on your outside or downhill ski. Photo 10

6. Adjust edge angle, leverage, and pressure throughout the turn to control the arc which your ski carves.

7. When you have turned to the direction you desire, adjust edge angle, pressure, and leverage to neutralize your turn. Be sure your skis track (no sideslipping) in the traverse.

Note: Your upper body has only maintained balance throughout this turn. It has not turned your skis. Your upper body follows your skis; it does not lead them.

chapter 8

Wedges: Aid to Precision Ski Control

Wedges, sometimes called "cants," are strips of tapered material thicker on one edge than the other, placed under a skier's boot sole to change the edge angle of his skis on the snow.

A majority of skiers, if they stand in their boots on a hard floor, will stand on the outside of their soles, as in Drawing 11.

(Drawing #11)

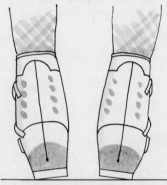

When the same skiers assume a straight running position on skis, their skis ride on the outside edges. When a wedge is placed between the bootsoles and the skis, the skis are flattened on the snow. Consider the following drawings.

The figures in the left column illustrate the primary problems of a skier whose natural stance is on his outside edges.

Look at Figure 1: In a straight running position, the skier is "stuck" on both outside edges; a turn cannot be initiated in either direction without catching an outside edge. Four compensations are possible:

    1)   Stem the outside ski by picking it up and moving it laterally until it is flat on the snow;

[56]

2) hop off the ground with both feet and move them laterally until the outside ski is flat;

3) simply carry the outside ski off the snow while turning on the inside ski;

4) ski knock-kneed, with your feet apart and your knees squeezed together.

(Drawing #12)

1. STRAIGHT RUNNING POSITION.

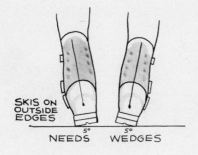

SKIS ON OUTSIDE EDGES
5° 5°
NEEDS WEDGES

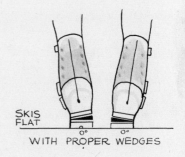

SKIS FLAT
0° 0°
WITH PROPER WEDGES

2. LEFT TURN.

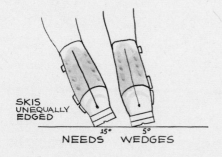

SKIS UNEQUALLY EDGED
15° 5°
NEEDS WEDGES

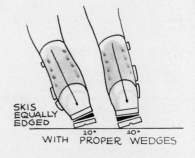

SKIS EQUALLY EDGED
10° 10°
WITH PROPER WEDGES

3. EDGE CHANGE – LEFT TURN TO RIGHT TURN.

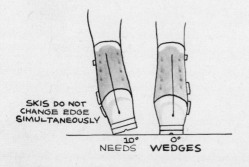

SKIS DO NOT CHANGE EDGE SIMULTANEOUSLY
10° 0°
NEEDS WEDGES

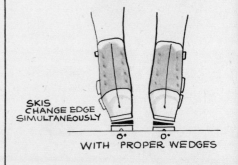

SKIS CHANGE EDGE SIMULTANEOUSLY
0° 0°
WITH PROPER WEDGES

A good racer, instinctively trying to maintain snow contact, will carve turns on his inside ski. A recreational skier, lacking the strength and balance to turn on his inside ski, will stem or hop. A consistently knock-kneed position is too awkward and uncomfortable to be useful.

There are thousands of perpetual stem turners in America—people who have taken lessons for years with hopes of becoming parallel skiers. Many of these people don't need lessons; they need wedges to flatten their skis in a natural stance. Without wedges, it is impossible for them to turn without stemming or hopping. The stem or hop is a necessary movement to accomplish edge change. Likewise there are thousands of racers who continually turn on their inside skis despite daily protests from their coaches. For a racer needing wedges, the inside ski offers the most efficient turn possible. His instinct to use it is correct.*

Look at Figure 2: In a moderate left turn, the downhill ski is insufficiently edged to produce an adequate carving response or to adequately resist sideslip. Weight on the downhill ski produces a skidding turn. The racer who cannot maintain a desired line while skidding is forced to turn on his inside ski, which is adequately edged to carve well and to resist sideslip.

For any skier needing wedges, the primary problem—and it exists in turns of all radii—is that his skis are always *unequally edged*. Because edge angle is a primary factor in determining the arc on which a ski turns, skis unequally edged can never make the same kind of turn. As the inside ski is edged more, it carves a tighter turn. To equalize, the outside ski must be skidded or must have greater twisting force applied, etc. An alternative solution is to stand on one ski only—either inside or outside.

By contrast, the properly wedged skier in Figures 2 and 3 can move easily from one ski to another or stand equally on both. As both skis are equally edged, equal turning forces are applied at every phase of a turn.

Look at Figure 3: At the time of edge change, the improperly wedged skier does not change edge simultaneously with both skis. To change edge he must displace his skis from under his plumb line; this detracts from optimum balance and economy of motion. By contrast, a properly wedged skier changes edges not only simultaneously,

---

* Coaches and ski instructors take note: When a racer or ski-school pupil continually makes the same "mistake" despite your instructions to the contrary, you must seek a solution other than their lack of coordination or understanding. That solution can almost always be found in equipment modification.

(Drawing #13)

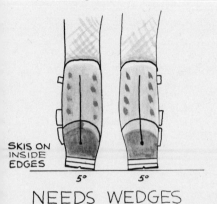
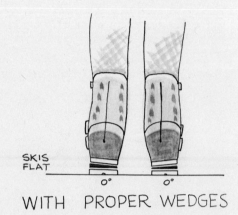

but also when both skis are directly under his plumb line. Balance and economy of motion are thus improved.

There is no requirement more basic for an efficient ski technique than having your skis change edge simultaneously, and having them equally edged at all points in a turn. Proper wedges assure that these requirements are met.

A majority of skiers stand naturally on their outside edges and require wedges mounted thick side inside, as in Drawing 12, page 57. Some skiers, however, stand naturally on their inside edges as in Drawing 13, above.

To flatten their skis on the snow these skiers require wedges mounted thick side outside. For these people the outside ski is edged more in each turn than the inside ski. This causes frequent crossing of the tips. Turns begin too quickly, the downhill ski turning more sharply than inward lean can balance for.

A skier who is too much on his inside edge often leans into turns as in Drawing 14.

This skier leans into the turn with his head and shoulders to maintain balance (bicycle-lean angle); and he moves his hip to the outside of the turn to reduce the edge angle of his outside ski. A skier with this problem always feels too much on edge; and there is no easy way to compensate.

To flatten his skis, his knees must be displaced *outward*. Reverse angulation (with hip away from the hill, as in Drawing 14) is required to stay in balance. This is uncomfortable and inefficient to say the least.

A racer who is too much on his inside edges has difficulty ending turns precisely. His downhill ski—because it is too severely edged—

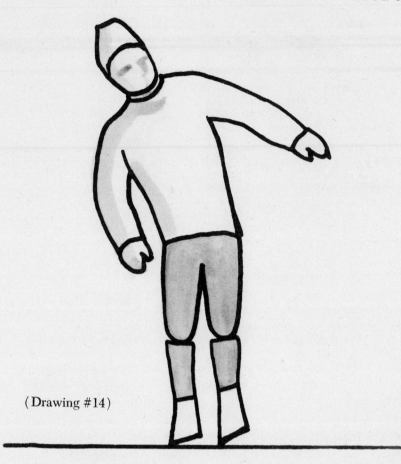

(Drawing #14)

has a strong tendency to overturn. Thus it is difficult to "neutralize" turns at the precise instant that provides optimum line and acceleration for each traverse.

Coaches and instructors working extensively with wedges should try skiing for one whole day with wedges that place them on their outside edges in a natural stance, and then ski another day with wedges that place them on their inside edges. Only then can they appreciate the many difficulties skiers have when improperly wedged. Also, they will more easily recognize the symptoms of other people with wedge needs. This experiment is instructive for racers and recreational skiers too. It helps them to appreciate and understand the effects wedges can have on their skiing.

Prior to 1972, most ski boots were made so that nearly all skiers stood naturally on their outside edges. Responding to the publicity given to wedges in 1970 and 1971, the boot-makers (especially of high-priced racing boots) built a more severe outward cant in their 1972 boots. The result was that many more people—at least a third of the 500 racers I tested—stand naturally on their inside edges in the new boots. Wedges mounted thick side outside must be used to balance these skiers on a flat ski.

Why Do So Many Skiers Need Wedges? Human leg bones are as varied in shape as human noses. Each person's leg and ankle structure produces a slightly different angle for the shin bone to rise from the floor in a natural stance. Boot-makers obviously cannot meet the exact needs of each customer.

How can you tell if you need wedges? For positive measurement, buckle your ski boots just as you do to ski. Stand on a smooth, hard, level surface with your feet the same distance apart as in your natural skiing stance. Are you on the outside or inside edges of your boot soles? If so, you need wedges. When you roll your knees to change from left edges to right edges do your soles flatten simultaneously, or do they change one before the other? If they flatten simultaneously, you don't need wedges. If they flatten one before the other, you do. Now roll your boot soles about 20 degrees on edge (use knee movement only), and have someone look under your soles to see if they are equally edged. If they aren't, you need wedges. Whatever variation occurs on a flat floor will be the same as the angle of your skis to the snow.

How Thick Should Your Wedges Be? By trial and error on a flat floor you can experiment with varying wedge thicknesses until both boots are flat in a natural stance, and edged equally in a turn. When you have exactly the right amount of wedge, you can stand in a relaxed, natural position and by moving just your knees one inch left and right cause both your boot soles to rock equally on their left and right edges. To feel precisely if their boot soles are flat, most racers stand in balance on both feet, but move just one knee—left and right—concentrating on the precise edging of one boot at a time. You may require a different amount of wedge on each foot; or a wedge for only one foot.

Good skiers, who are sensitive to the feel of their boots and of their skis on the snow, can tell very precisely when they are perfectly wedged by the above method. Skiers who are unaccustomed to sensing edge angle will be less confident.

There are various machines like the CB SPORTS EDGE EXACTOR and the KENNEDY COMPUTOR that measure wedge needs. These machines have two free-swinging treadles on which you stand. The amount the treadle rolls off level is calibrated to indicate your wedge need. (See Photos 11A, B, and 12.)

MALCOLM REISS

11A and B. The CB Sports Edge Exactor is the best machine available for measuring wedge needs. The photo opposite shows a skier whose natural stance is on his outside edges. To level his skis, wedges must be placed thickside-inside. This skier requires a 5° wedge under his left boot and a 7° wedge under his right boot.

CB SPORTS and KENNEDY both produce wedges in varying thicknesses that are compatible to their testing machines. Only the CB EDGE EXACTOR is calibrated in degrees of arc, which is the best way to measure a wedge. The EDGE EXACTOR is the most accurate measuring device now available. Experienced coaches can measure wedge needs to ½-degree tolerances. Wedges are available in a range from 1 to 8 degrees. It is advisable to check EDGE EXACTOR readings by standing on a flat floor with the prescribed amount of wedge under your boots. If the wedge is exactly right, your boot soles will be flat as described in the preceding paragraphs on flat-floor measurement. This double check insures greater accuracy in determining your wedge needs.

When mounting wedges on your skis, it is important to place them under the bindings. This is necessary to have the bindings operate on

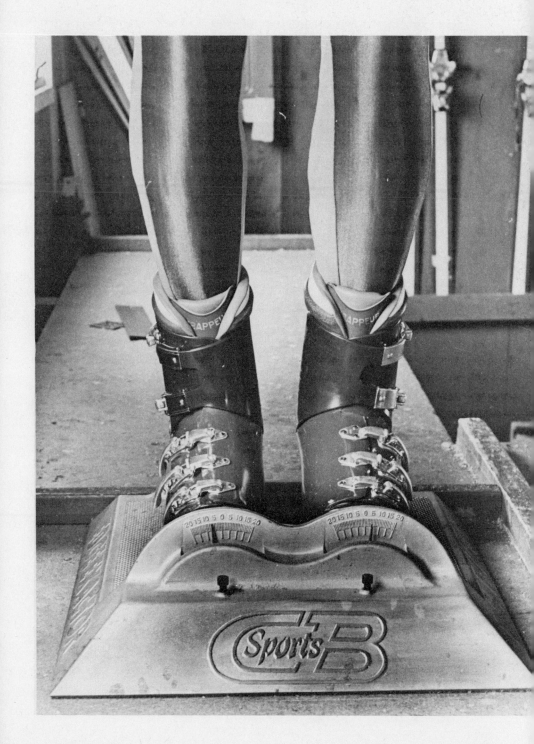

Photos 11A, B

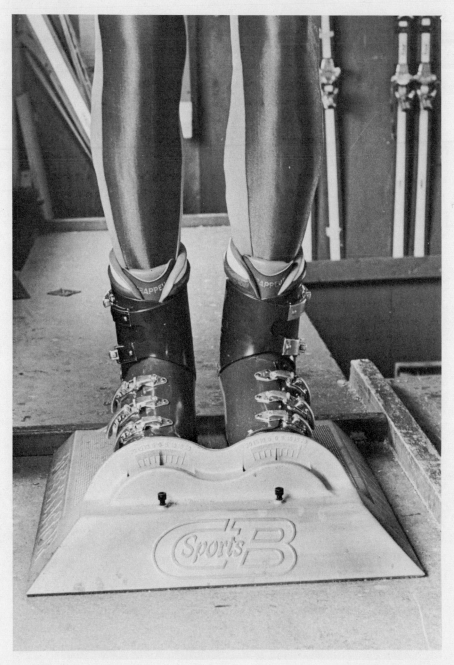

12. *With the 7° and 5° wedges placed under the racer's boots while he stands on the Exactor, a level stance is shown by the needle indicators.*

a plane parallel to your boot soles. Cut the wedges in two pieces to prohibit buckling as the ski bends, and to save material. The front piece must extend from the front of your toe piece to the ball of your foot. It must cover or go under your antifriction plate so the wedge angle is effective where the ball of your foot contacts the ski. The back piece of wedge goes under your heel unit.

There are other ways to accomplish the same result. One is to re-shape your boot soles with a belt sander. This is advisable only where less than ⅛-inch of wedging (about 2 degrees) is necessary, as more extensive sanding weakens the sole. If you reduce the thickness of the outside edge of your sole, the inside edge must be equally planed on the top of the sole where it contacts the safety binding. (See Drawing 15.)

If shaded area A is sanded off the bottom, shaded area B must be cut from the heel and toe to maintain the constant sole thickness required by safety bindings.

A few boots, like Rosemont, can be individually canted by tilting the entire boot shaft. This may be a correct method of canting to some degree, but your ankle should not be unnaturally bent in your boot.

Photo
12

(Drawing #15)

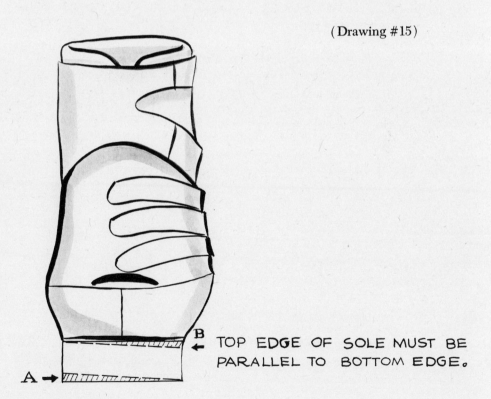

B
←
A →

TOP EDGE OF SOLE MUST BE PARALLEL TO BOTTOM EDGE.

Some wedges are made to be placed inside your boot—much like an arch support, but usually placed under your heel. These wedges do not appreciably change the angle of your ski edge on the snow. They only constrict your foot in the boot. *They are a hoax, and they should not be used.* They change only the relationship between the sole of your foot and the boot lining. Your heel bone and lower shin bone are still restricted at the same angle in your boot shaft. These wedges are medically unsound, and do not even achieve the purpose for which they are advertised. Wedges placed inside a boot are useful only to cure problems such as flat feet and fallen arches. Such wedges should *always* be prescribed by a doctor.

Whenever you get new boots, you must be rechecked for wedge needs. Any determination of wedge needs is correct only for the boots you are wearing *when checked.* As those boots break in, or break down, they should be rechecked. It is especially important to recheck after the first two weeks of skiing, as boots may change by 2 degrees while breaking in. Racers sensitive to wedge needs will feel the change in the performance of their skis when their boots change as little as ½-degree.

It is important before checking wedge needs that you sand irregularities from your boot soles. If you place even the most expensive new boots on a flat table, you will find that the soles are not perfectly flat. On some boots the heel and toe are torsionally twisted on different planes. Other boots have soles like a rocker. Such boots give unreliable readings on an edge exactor, or on a flat floor. A permanently mounted bench or floor-model belt sander is the best tool for flattening boot soles.

Many people may feel that all this talk about wedging is much ado about nothing. Believe me, it is more than worth the effort! The improved efficiencies in balance, economy of motion, and precision ski control are much greater than anyone expects until they have skied with exactly correct wedges. For recreational skiers, wedging to 2 degrees accuracy (about ⅛-inch in the width of a boot sole) is acceptable, but 1 degree is preferable. For racers, I insist on wedging to ½-degree accuracy, about $\frac{1}{32}$-inch in the width of a boot sole.

Racers who have a particularly sensitive feel for edge change and balance relationships can identify wedge needs as small as ¼-degree when skiing on hard snow. To experiment with such small adjustments, racers at Burke Mountain place thin strips of cloth tape on their skis. Four strips are equal to one degree. Some racers are sensitive to changes of a single piece of tape. Permanent adjustments of wedge needs less than 1 degree are made by sanding boot soles.

Almost all boys should be wedged so their skis are perfectly flat in a natural skiing stance. Most girls should be wedged so their skis are

½ to 1 degree on their outside edges. This difference is required by the wider hip structure and resultant difference in knee joints common to girls. When girls simultaneously bend their knees and move them laterally to angulate, their knees "collapse" to the inside. This causes more edge angle and a sharper turn on their outside ski than inward lean can compensate for. (Equivalent lateral knee movement by a boy causes greater hip movement in the same direction—and provides greater inward lean at the center of body mass.) Girls who are wedged "flat" exhibit the same technical and balance problems that boys show when wedged too much on their inside edges.

I am convinced that the variation in performance by some international-class racers from one season to another has often been caused by changes in wedge needs resulting from a change of boots. Even within a single season, racers have periods of success and failure which are hard to explain. Some of these changes are caused by boots breaking in and changing wedge needs.

I have seen skiers in my own program winning races in December, then falling behind in January. A simple change of 1 degree in wedge needs (required by boot break-in) has put these racers back in the winner's circle. That 1-degree difference, particularly if the skier is too much on his inside edges, can be worth more than two or three seconds per race.

part II

Your Body

Preface

Analysis of body positions and function has for too many years been prejudiced by uncompromising devotion to particular ski systems: Arlburg, Allais, Austrian, French, American, etc. Certain elements of these popular techniques have been more stylish than functional. Allegiance to them has been more emotional than rational, and in many cases has been commercial.

Ski technicians must focus their attention on body mechanics, balance, and economy of motion. Coaches must learn from the experience of other sports—like gymnastics, figure-skating, water-skiing, track and field, fancy diving, modern dance, etc.

For example:

POSTURE—The most important element in developing and maintaining a smooth efficient running style is an upright posture. This is just as true for the sprinter as for the jogger. Ideally, when you are running, your posture should be so erect that a plumb line could be dropped from your ear lobe straight down through the line of the shoulder, the line of the hip and then on to the ground. Unfortunately, many people, including athletes, seem to feel it is necessary to lean forward in order to generate maximum thrust while running. This is wrong. A forward lean might be useful for someone trying to bash down a wall with his head, but in running it merely gives the leg muscles a lot of unnecessary work. When the upper body is permitted to rotate forward beyond the center of gravity—that is to say, forward of the straight up-and-down line—the lower body must compensate by rotating back behind the center of gravity.

Bill Bowerman
Track Coach, UNIVERSITY OF OREGON
"The Secrets of Speed"
Sports Illustrated, August 2, 1971

chapter 9

Maintaining Good Balance

To ski as the best racers do, you must understand that the primary function of the upper body in modern ski technique is to maintain balance.

UPPER-BODY MOVEMENTS OR POSITIONS THAT CONTRIBUTE TO QUICK-NESS, AGILITY, AND BALANCE ARE CORRECT.

UPPER-BODY MOVEMENTS OR POSITIONS THAT DETRACT FROM QUICK-NESS, AGILITY, AND BALANCE ARE WRONG.

You must develop a natural and balanced stance on your skis. What body positions contribute most to good balance?

1.   Stand nearly erect—as the figures in Drawing 16 illustrate.
Note that in both the high and low hip positions the back remains almost vertical and the hip bone (which carries the weight of the upper body) is balanced over the heels. Many skiers, especially young racers, bend too much at the waist. This bend puts the head and shoulders forward—so the fanny must go back to achieve balance. This position detracts seriously from the agility, balance, and strength, of a skier.

To prove this, stand in sneakers on a smooth floor. With your waist bent 70 degrees (and keeping your feet together) jump ten times as rapidly as possible from side to side. Then stand erect, and jump from side to side. The erect stance permits far quicker movement. You feel lighter on your feet when erect. Consider the importance of this quickness when skiing in moguls or running slalom. Simple exercises like this demonstrate the importance of basic physics and body mechanics. When your waist is excessively bent, your head and shoulders literally hang on your back muscles. When your back muscles are under this strain, leg coordination is seriously impaired.

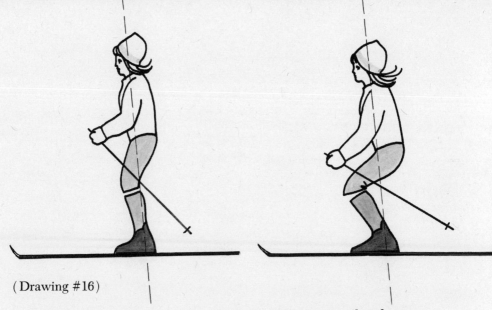

(Drawing #16)

Next time you see a good tennis match note the position the players assume to receive service. They bend their knees, but keep their upper bodies almost erect. They do not "jack" at the waist. Quicker movement is possible from the erect position. Football line-backers use a similar stance.

2. Keep your hips over your heel bones. As your upper body weight is carried by your hips, this produces the easiest balance and support of your body weight by your back structure. As your hips move back of the balance line, you must bend at the waist to move your head and shoulders forward. This bent-waist position causes the loss of agility discussed previously, and places more of your body weight on your muscle systems. Consider again the tennis player receiving service: As he bends his knees (to provide spring) he moves them *forward* so his hips remain over his heels. Hips over heels assures optimum quickness, agility, and balance.

3. Stand "square" on your skis—i.e. with your body (hips and shoulders) facing in the same direction as your skis.

An exaggerated reverse shoulder position, taught for so long by Austrian and American ski schools, is an absolutely ridiculous way to ski. It makes no more sense to ski on a sustained traverse with your upper body facing in a direction different from your feet than it does to walk, skate, or bicycle that way. All skiers will use "reverse shoulder" (and less reverse hip) at certain times in closely linked turns when it is a *natural* motion of anticipation or an efficient way to *decrease* upper-body motion. But as a sustained traverse position, it is the greatest piece of sports humbug ever sold by a group of "experts" to a gullible public. If you have been taught in ski school to force your body into this twisted traverse position, do yourself a

[73]

favor: Just stand on one side of your favorite trail—stand erect and naturally—bend your knees slightly, and then traverse across the trail. Don't bend or twist your upper body. Just stand naturally and ski. You will feel a tremendous sense of relaxation and good balance. If you stand square on your skis—the French and Swiss have done it for years—you will ski far more comfortably than most American and Austrian ski instructors do.

4.   Carry your hands comfortably in front of you, at equal elevation and a comfortable distance apart. Whenever possible, your hands should move in mirror image: They should be equal width, equal altitude, equal reach (forward and back). From this "home position," small balance adjustments can be made, as required, by moving your arms independently.

In any sport requiring balance (ballet, figure-skating, gymnastics) the hands and arms are the primary instrument for making balance adjustments. Only if the "home position" is in perfect balance can the hands be moved to make balance compensations required by other body movements.

Photos
13A, 13B

Many skiers lift the outside arm to initiate turns, or use other arm motions to create rotation and weight changes. These are incorrect uses of the hands. Your lower body—ankles, knees, hips—should be used to cause your skis to turn. Your arms should be free to serve as a balance tool, adjusting to shocks from terrain change, etc.

PHOTOPRESS

13A and B. The French star Patrick Russell, made famous by the popular press for his "sitting-back" techniques, illustrates the real genius of his skiing. Russell has the quietest upper body and most perfectly disciplined hands on the World Cup circuit. He is almost always in perfect balance—able to concentrate on feeling the snow and using his skis to create turning forces. In these two pictures, both a high and low hip position are seen. In the first picture, he has reached the compression point of his turn, and is just ready to set his edges for the following traverse. He has probably dropped his hips to create a very soft touch on the snow at the time of edge-set. Note that his hands, which are very low, are not tense. His arms are relaxed—with a slight break evident at the the elbow.

In the bottom photo, Russell is taking a lateral step in slalom. His erect stance gives him great strength and agility—allowing for a very quick step to be made. Both arms are rising in unison. This motion provides additional pressure on the right ski while the arms are rising. When the upward motion of the arms is arrested, an unweighting will occur. Russell will time this unweighting to coincide with his weight shift to the left ski. Note that Russell is in a position of neutral leverage—his hips well balanced over his heels—in both the high and low hip positions.

A↑ ↓B

If you need an arm motion to unweight your skis (a valid movement sometimes) use both arms in parallel movement. That way they provide unweighting without otherwise changing the balance of your body. If one arm is used it tilts head or shoulders and disturbs the balance of your whole body. If one arm moves excessively forward or back, it draws the attached shoulder with it, causing an undesired twist of your upper body and often of your hips too.

Keep your elbows off your hips, so that you have unrestricted movement of your arms. When your elbows are on your hips, they can move only one way—out. By keeping your elbows free of your body, they can move in or out. Do not hold your arms straight. This allows adjusting movements only in one direction—bending. Balance adjustment must be possible both bending and extending your arm.

5. Plant your poles so as to require as little arm movement as possible. The secret is to keep your knuckles pointing straight ahead. Don't roll your wrists out. For each pole plant, your pole should be brought forward by wrist action only. After planting your pole, your hand should go straight ahead over the pole. In a proper pole plant the arm

PHOTOPRESS

13C. *Jean-Noel Augert, World Cup Slalom Champion, is seen here in a typical position—hips high, back erect, applying forward leverage at the start of his turn. He has "turned his back to the pole" to get a tighter line, but his hips are turned much less than his shoulders; and his hands are in a conservative position. His arms are comfortably bent— allowing for balance adjustment both ways. He has neither lifted his outside arm, as so many racers do to unweight, nor dropped his inside hand to duck his shoulder by the pole. In this balanced position, he is able to concentrate on the carving action of his skis.*

13D. *Leslie Orton, 16-year-old Junior National Giant Slalom Champion in 1972, exhibits a wide stance, erect upper body, almost balanced hands and arms. Those who saw her run commented, "She was wonderfully smooth." Do quiet upper-body positions result from effective use of the ski to create turning power? Or does the effective use of the ski make possible the quiet and balanced upper body? The question is like the old adage about the chicken or the egg. One is not possible without the other. As racers develop increasing skills at using their skis to create turning forces, they require fewer upper-body motions to initiate or to complete turns. As they learn to discipline their upper bodies, they are better able to feel the snow, and to make more effective use of their skis. At Burke Mountain, we concentrate on teaching kids to feel the snow, and to use the design potential of their skis. The quiet body positions develop naturally as each racer acquires the skills needed to carve turns.*

Photos 13C, 13D

MALCOLM REISS

scarcely moves; by limiting arm movement, upper-body balance is disturbed as little as possible.

I almost never tell a racer to do something with his upper body to create a turn. I confine upper-body coaching to eliminating inefficient movements—wild arm motions, rolling wrists out on pole plants, bending and straightening at the waist, ducking the head, etc. Skiers should strive for simplified pole plants, for quieting of the hands and arms, for an erect and square upper-body stance. I never tell a racer, "Begin the turn with your outside arm," or "Rotate your shoulder at X point in the turn." I simply urge racers to achieve economy of motion in their upper bodies. Consistent balance in the upper body allows for dynamic and precise use of the knees and feet to control turns.

Undisciplined racers are constantly delayed in their turns while trying to get their upper bodies into a position which allows them to turn their feet. Think for a moment how often when you are skiing your mind says "turn now" and your feet are ready to turn—but a hand or shoulder is so askew that your upper body is sufficiently off balance to prohibit the lower-body movements you desire. This dilemma is constant for all but the most disciplined skiers.

Photos
13E,13F

The secret of precise and efficient skiing is to discipline unnecessary motion from your upper body so you are always in balance and can move instantly in any direction. To achieve this disciplined stance may at first require conscious effort to unlearn old habits. As you learn to "feel the snow" and to turn your skis by edge angle and pressure change, balanced body positions become natural and unself-conscious. When you reach this point, skiing becomes a natural and free activity. It's a beautiful feeling!

Each of the six photos on pages 75, 76, 77, and 79 illustrates a correct stance on snow skis: an erect upper body, hands in balance at equal altitude and spread, nearly square hip and shoulder positions.

MALCOLM REISS

13E and F. Two young skiers from the Junior Racing Program at Stowe, Vermont, show the results of good coaching. Jeff Stone, age 13, and Dani Shaw, 11, ski in good balance. Both youngsters are balanced over their downhill skis—and are ready to step onto their uphill skis for the next turn. Modern racing techniques are learned quickly and naturally by children whose boots and skis are as responsive as those used by World Cup racers. Rossignol and K2 make especially good skis for racers weighing as little as 60 pounds.

chapter 10

Longitudinal Balance: Boots and Heel Lifts

A skier must be balanced on two axes: longitudinal (forward-back) and lateral (left-right).

Ski boots, because they have a stiff shaft which immobilizes the ankle, can seriously hinder a skier's balance. Skiing, like running, requires that we bend our knees, in varying degrees. Standing barefoot, or in soft shoes, the ankle joint rolls forward and back as the knees bend. This helps a person to remain in balance with his hips over his heels. The six figures in Drawing 17 illustrate problems of forward and backward balance in snow skiing.

Figure 1 shows a completely erect stance. The body is in balance.

Figure 2 shows a balanced stance with a slight knee bend. This is a comfortable, neutral position for many athletic activities.

Figure 3 shows a balanced stance with moderate knee bend.

Figure 4 shows a balanced and comfortable stance with extreme knee bend.

Figure 5 shows an unbalanced stance with extreme knee bend.

Figure 6 shows a balanced but strained stance with extreme knee bend. An excessive bend at the waist is required to maintain balance.

[80]

(Drawing #17)

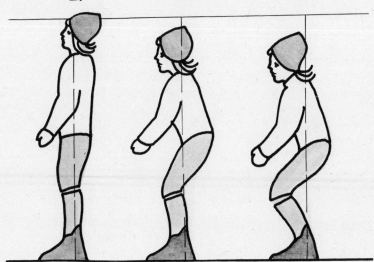

1.	2.	3.
ERECT STANCE	BALANCED	BALANCED
	SLIGHT KNEE BEND	MODERATE KNEE BEND

4.	5.	6.
BALANCED	UNBALANCED	BALANCED
EXTREME KNEE BEND	90° KNEE BEND	90° KNEE BEND

Please note the various degrees of bend at the ankle joint in each of these illustrations. Now consider what would happen if you skied in boots with a vertical shaft. You would be limited to positions 1, 5, or 6. Number 1, the stiff-kneed position, is obviously not useful. Number 5, the sitting-back position, places great strain on your thigh and abdominal muscles, and applies excessive pressure to the tails of your skis. It is terribly out of balance. Number 6, though balanced on the skis, places excessive strain on both thigh and back muscles. It is hardly a comfortable position in which to spend a day skiing.

If you wish to ski in a relaxed, balanced position, you must function in the movement range between positions 2 and 4. Note the angle of forward lean at the ankle. In Figure 2 it is 10 degrees. In Figure 4 it is 35 degrees. How much forward lean should be built into the shaft of our boots? This is not an academic question. It is a vital concern to any skier who wants to maintain longitudinal balance. One alternative is to build boots that will flex between 10 and 35 degrees. This alternative is unacceptable, as boots that are soft do not permit precise application of leverage to the ski. A compromise must be made between optimum ski control and optimum balance. *This compromise will not be the same for every skier.*

The first variable is the aggressiveness, strength, and technical skill of the skier. A middle-aged week-end skier with average parallel ability will ski 90 per cent of the time between positions 2 and 3. He has neither the strength nor the technical need to bend his knees 90 degrees. This skier will require an ankle lean between 10 and 20 degrees. He would be most uncomfortable and unbalanced in a locked-hinge racing boot with 25 degrees forward lean. A boot with 15 to 20 degrees forward lean would be adequate.

An international-class racer, on the other hand, requires maximum lateral knee flexibility for severe edging. This requires a deeper bend in the knees. He has the strength to ski between positions 3 and 4 for extended periods of time. This skier requires, for optimum balance, a forward ankle lean in the range from 20 to 40 degrees. How much forward lean should be built into his boots? Thirty degrees would be a mathematical compromise, but in practice, that has proven too much. Even the stiffest boots still have a little give—mostly forward. So we compromise at something less than the midpoint. Let's say 25 degrees provides optimum balance, comfort, and edge control for the racer. In fact, most modern racing boots provide a forward lean of 22 to 26 degrees when mounted on the most popular bindings. When extreme leverage is applied to these boots, they flex to a shaft angle as great as 40 degrees and as little as 15.

There is much dispute among racers, coaches, and boot-makers as to how stiff boots should be. Some flexibility in a boot contributes to balance by permitting ankle flexibility; it also improves a skier's "feel" for the snow. Excessive flexibility, however, reduces control over the ski, which in the end also reduces balance. The problem is the same as that faced by suspension engineers working with racing cars. The springing must be firm enough to provide control, but not so firm as to destroy a car's ability to absorb road bumps and terrain variations. It is not unrealistic to think of ski boots as a suspension system connecting a skier's body to his skis. There is also much dispute as to how high boots should be. Many racers went to excessively high and stiff boots in early 1971, then finished the season in lower boots. Continued experimentation will lead to a happy compromise. Individuals, of course, will always have preferences both stiffer and softer than the norms.

If we build racing boots with a 22-degree shaft angle, what degree will the angle be when these boots are mounted on a pair of skis? (See Drawing 18.)

In the upper drawing the bindings tilt the boot forward 4 degrees. In the lower drawing the bindings tilt the boot forward 2 degrees. Two degrees is a big difference; it can put a skier far off balance. If a racer was in perfect balance with a Marker Rotomat, and he changed to Salomon bindings, he would be sitting back; he would be off balance; and he would be applying pressure excessively to the tails of his skis. Also note that pressure is applied further back on the ski with the Salomon binding. I have seen racers change bindings in this manner and fall apart as competitive skiers. They can't keep their skis in a long turn because they can't maintain adequate pressure on the tips of their skis; they are continually off balance to the rear. What can be done? There are two choices: Go back to the original bindings, or use a "heel lift." *

A heel lift is any piece of material mounted under a boot heel so as to tilt the boot forward. (See Drawing 19.)

It may be attached to the sole of the boot or mounted under the binding. A size 8 boot will have about 2 degrees additional forward lean when you put a ⅛-inch lift under the heel. To experiment tape a piece of plastic, leather, or rubber under your heels. A little ingenuity will allow you to try heel lifts with most bindings. If your boots have too much forward lean you can use a thicker antifriction plate under the

---

* I do not imply that the Salomon is inferior. It is simply different. Some racers might have too much forward lean with the Marker; they would be in better balance with the Salomon.

(Drawing #18)

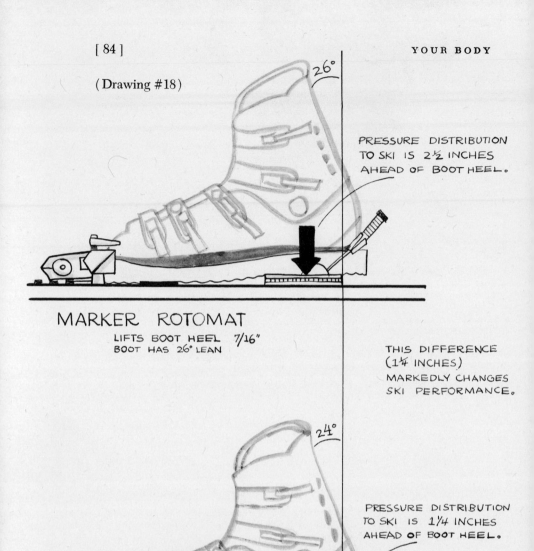

26°

PRESSURE DISTRIBUTION
TO SKI IS 2½ INCHES
AHEAD OF BOOT HEEL.

MARKER ROTOMAT
LIFTS BOOT HEEL 7/16"
BOOT HAS 26° LEAN

THIS DIFFERENCE
(1¼ INCHES)
MARKEDLY CHANGES
SKI PERFORMANCE.

24°

PRESSURE DISTRIBUTION
TO SKI IS 1¼ INCHES
AHEAD OF BOOT HEEL.

SOLOMON 505
LIFTS BOOT HEEL 5/16"
BOOT HAS 24° LEAN

THE SAME BOOT WITH A 22° SHAFT
ANGLE PRODUCES A 24- OR 26-DEGREE
LEAN WHEN MOUNTED ON DIFFERENT
BINDINGS.

(Drawing #19)

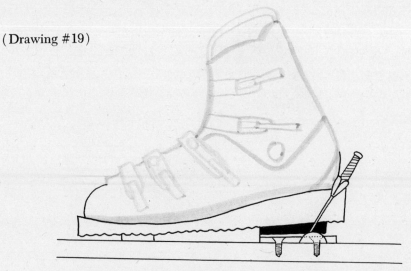

HEEL LIFT OVER BINDING
(TEMPORARY)

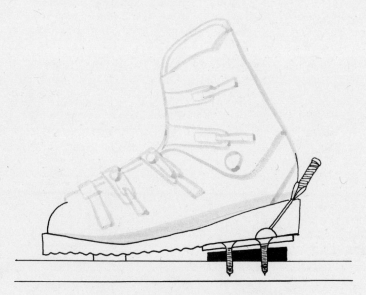

HEEL LIFT UNDER BINDING
(PERMANENT)

ball of your foot to rock the boot backward. Don't try to change forward lean by putting heel lifts *inside your boots.* They are ineffective, as your legs are still restricted by the boot shells.

It is impossible for boot manufacturers to provide the exact amount of forward lean each individual requires. Racers need more than recreational skiers. Thus, racing boots are built with more forward lean. Many young racers, however, have lower-priced boots with insufficient lean for the racing techniques they are trying to use.

It is my firm belief that many racers even on the World Cup Circuit are not perfectly balanced on their skis. Most of the American girls in 1971, for instance, were in Lange Competition boots, and the boots just didn't have sufficient forward lean for the low hip positions the girls were using. They were off balance to the rear. This impaired the performance of the girls' team. Most of the boys had Lange "Supercomps," a newer custom boot with 4 or 5 degrees additional forward lean. The success of the supercomps verified the need for greater forward lean; but few coaches in the world made the necessary adjustments for older boots. Certainly, the Supercomps had too much lean for some skiers who use a more erect technique, or whose body builds (light buttocks and heavier chest) allow them to ski in balance with their hips a little further back.

The point I am making is simple: *Fine adjustments in forward lean angle of boots are absolutely necessary for any racer or recreational skier who wishes to ski in optimum balance.* Each skier must find his own balance point by trial and error. This takes some effort; but it's worth it. You only have to see the expression on some youngster's faces after their first turns with proper heel lifts to appreciate how significantly longitudinal balance affects technique. The kids beam with delight. They always comment: "I feel much quicker—much lighter on my feet." They are in better balance!

chapter 11

Wedges and Balance

In Chapter 8 we discussed the importance of wedges to improve precision ski control. Correct wedging makes equally important contributions to balance.

If you need wedges you suffer a decrease in balance because:

1. You must unweight abnormally to initiate turns (Excessive body motion disturbs a quiet, neutral stance on your skis.)

2. You are more liable to skidding in turns and traverses. (Any skidding activity is unstable.)

3. Edge change cannot occur while your body is in perfect lateral balance over your ski(s).

These problems are clearly illustrated by one-ski turns. Imagine yourself on a smooth, gentle slope, making linked turns on one ski. If you are properly wedged, you can ski straight down the fall line as in Drawing 20. Your ski will be flat on the snow when directly under your plumb line.

If you need wedges when you stand straight, your ski will be on edge as in Figure 2. To flatten that ski in a straight running position, you must angulate as in Figure 3. Angulation at the moment of edge change requires undesirable upper-body movement. By using proper wedges, as in Figure 4, you can stand as straight on your skis as Figure 1.

Modern ski technique involves a continual shifting of weight from one outside ski to the other in succeeding turns. Each turn requires the same balance adjustments over the outside ski as those analyzed in the one-ski exercises above.

One-foot turns are stock in trade for racers, and should be for recreational skiers. Simple step turns offer easy direction changes with minimal upper-body movement. Because a skier's full weight is applied

ONE-SKI TURNS

NEEDS NO WEDGES

NEEDS WEDGES

FIG. 1

FIG. 2

SKI FLAT WHEN
STANDING STRAIGHT.

SKI ON OUTSIDE
EDGE WHEN
STANDING STRAIGHT.

NEEDS WEDGES

PROPERLY WEDGED

FIG. 3

FIG. 4

ANGULATION
REQUIRED TO
FLATTEN SKI.

SKI FLAT WHEN
STANDING
STRAIGHT.

to one ski, the ski is easily bent into reverse camber, allowing effortless carved turns at slow speeds. Step turns should be taught very early to beginning skiers, as they are the easiest slow-speed turn (except the snowplow, which is in a sense a one-ski turn). One reason that one-foot turns have not been taught to beginners is that they are so difficult for people who need wedges. Eighty per cent of all skiers do. Many instructors, therefore, as well as their students, are restricted from performing one-ski maneuvers in adequate balance. With proper wedges, balance is easy, and the whole range of one-ski maneuvers can be used by beginning and intermediate skiers. For the expert skier, the proper balance on one ski which wedges provide greatly improves his precision and control in all turns initiated with a stepping motion or a major weight transfer from one foot to the other.

chapter 12

The Function of Your Upper Body in Most Ski Turns

The primary purpose of your upper body is to provide balance—by anticipation and by reaction. Reactionary balance occurs in all turns: If you carve a turn to the left, your upper body is thrown to the right (outside the turning arc) by centrifugal force. Your body *subconsciously* and *automatically* leans into the turn to maintain balance. This action, if not consciously prohibited, will occur whether you are running, walking, skating, skiing, or surfing.

Anticipatory balance is more complex. As you become confident of the moves your skis and feet will make, you can increasingly anticipate turns by leaning to the inside with your body. Use angulation—not head and shoulder lean! In long, smooth turns, body lean progresses in close syncronization with the turn. But where quick turns are made, your body must clearly anticipate the turning of your feet or skis. As you improve your anticipation, you extend the range of what you can do with your feet. In this anticipation, your body may or may not contribute turning force to your skis. Usually it does not. Inward lean or angulation prior to a turn does contribute edge angle to your skis. This satisfies my demand that to carve turns a ski must be edged first, and then turned. The same movement that edges your skis provides the bicycle-lean angle required to be in balance for the turn. I can best illustrate this with an example.

In 1971, David Currier (now on the National Team) was training giant slalom at Burke Mountain. On a flat, fast section of the course, two gates were set thirty feet apart which required a 15-degree direction change. At each gate there was a sharp rut, ten inches deep.

Currier approached the first gate on a very straight line, and just prior to hitting the rut he leaned about 30 degrees left with his entire upper body. Then he made a quick knee motion forward and left that drove his skis into the rut, and created a quick turn of 15 degrees. David was thrown into the air by the rut, but when he regained snow contact, he was in perfect balance and precisely on line to the next gate. The beauty of this turn was that after the explosive move of his skis, David came back onto the snow in perfect balance for the succeeding turn. *With his initial body lean, he had perfectly anticipated the dynamic action of his feet and skis—their change of direction and speed.*

What David demonstrated to an extreme degree was the process of anticipating the balance requirement of the turn his feet were about to make.

On steep terrain, making turns well across the fall line, racers often lean downhill and turn their upper bodies before turning their skis. This movement—inward lean and rotation in the direction of the turn —is often called "anticipation." It is much like water-ski slalom, where you lean first and then the ski turns under you. When you learn to use them, snow skis will do the same thing.

I believe that almost all that has been written about jet turns, avalement, sitting back, swallowing, anticipation turns, etc. can be reduced to "balancing your upper body for what your feet are going to do, or have quickly done."

I could use a hundred pages to present sequence pictures analyzing the variety of body motions used in modern turns. Joubert and others have done this most carefully, and their work is certainly useful to students of body mechanics; but I don't think many of these studies help the average skier to make better turns. If you had to think about all the body motions some ski writers describe, you'd have a nervous breakdown. When you do an "anticipation" turn, you don't think about rotating 15 degrees, dropping your left arm six inches, bending your knees 20 degrees, drawing your hips forward with stomach and thigh muscles, etc. You just lean downhill enough to be in balance when your feet turn as sharply as you plan to turn them. If you accelerate your skis, you may wind up sitting back. Then you must draw your body forward again to a balanced position. If you expect an accelerating movement from your skis, you anticipate that by adjusting your stance forward at the initiation of the turn. After the acceleration of your skis, you can thus be in balance—not sitting too far back. There are no static positions you must learn. Every turn is different! Your upper-body motion does not create turns—it adjusts for them, whether before or after the turns.

Only practice and experimentation can teach you the exact amount of movement required to balance your body for the infinite variety of turns you can make. You learn by doing! But you must first understand that balance is the primary upper-body function in snow skiing. To illustrate this, I have racers, on easy terrain, lean as far as possible to one side, and then turn their skis so quickly they don't lose their balance and fall. This exercise teaches the limits of angulation they can achieve and the sharpness of turns they can make in good balance.

The attempts of ski magazines to analyze modern ski turns by describing upper-body positions and movements have often been misleading. The best skiers they photograph have progressed beyond body-oriented techniques. But the writers who analyze see mostly upper-body positions; and they think those positions are synonymous with technique. The writers must learn to study skis and knees. Only then will they stop confusing readers who are trying to imitate racing styles. The styles are too free—and the turns too varied—to be learned from body-position studies. To ski as the racers do, you must learn to feel the snow and to carve turns with your skis as this book instructs. Correct upper-body positions will then follow naturally. Those positions will be relaxed, natural, erect, square. Your body will move as naturally when you ski as when you run.

part III
Physics and Skiing

chapter 13

Efficiency

Improved performance in almost all sports depends on three factors: Improved physical training (strength, endurance, coordination); improved equipment (lighter, stronger, more responsive, etc.); and improved techniques.

To improve technique is to develop more efficient body movements to accomplish specific goals. All sports offer a continuing challenge to develop more efficient body movements. In sports like skiing, changes in equipment design frequently demand new developments in technique. In sports like swimming and running, the variables in body motion are much less complicated than in skiing. Most progress in those sports is governed by superior conditioning, though some technical advances are still being made. In all sports, coaches must adjust efficiency norms to the variables of body build which each competitor has. For instance, despite the great amount of study given to hitting baseballs, no two major-league stars have quite the same stance or swing pattern. No player has successfully copied the style of Stan Musial or Ted Williams. Jack Nicklaus' golf swing is different from Arnold Palmer's. Each, however, has found the most efficient swing for his particular body build. This fact offers ski coaches a lesson in humility: *The most efficient technique for one racer may be quite different from what is best for another racer.* (Note the difference in body positions of Leith Lende and Sara Pendleton in Photos 7A and B.)

Although there must be room for diverse techniques, all skiers are confined, finally, by the unchangeable laws of physics. Gravity, momentum, centrifugal force, resistance, motion vectors—these and other identifiable factors of physics determine the activity of skiers. A complete student of skiing should understand as much of the relevant physics as possible. An excellent treatise on ski mechanics by Ed Wyman appears in the 1970 edition of *The Official American Ski Technique* (pages 57–89). Although Mr. Wyman describes mostly skidded turns made with excessive body motions, his analysis of momentum, resistance, and resultant vectors is useful, and is applicable to all turns whether carved or skidded.

What I want to emphasize here is that *efficiency* must be the primary goal of skiing technique. *Economy of motion* must be considered in all movements. In the words of a work simplification expert: we must "Work Smarter, Not Harder."

In every part of this book, I stress the need for balanced, quiet, disciplined upper-body movements. There is an inescapable relationship between these requirements and efficiency in skiing.

To fully appreciate this, you must consider the *time* involved for every movement of your hands, arms, or shoulders; and consider the *distance* you travel over the snow in this time. Study the following chart:

		1 second	⅒ second	⅟₁₀₀ second
At Slalom Speed	21 mph	30 feet	3 feet	3½ inches
At Giant Slalom Speed	41 mph	60 feet	6 feet	7 inches
At Downhill Speed	61 mph	90 feet	9 feet	11 inches

It takes about ³⁄₁₀ of a second to move one hand from hip level to shoulder level and return. In that ³⁄₁₀ second, a slalom skier travels nine feet; a giant slalom skier goes eighteen feet. If the start of a turn is delayed by that amount, a skier is seriously off line. Ten inches or twenty—the distance traveled in ³⁄₁₀₀ second—is a serious matter to Class A racers.

For the recreational skier, these time–distance figures are equally important. To begin turns at a precise place on the snow is often necessary, especially when skiing in moguls or on narrow trails. If you lose your balance for just one second, you travel twenty to thirty feet at recreational speeds.

All skiers know the frustration of trying to start a turn when one arm is askew, or they are otherwise off balance. The initiation of the turn is delayed. Precise control at any part of a turn is sacrificed for a lineal distance corresponding to the time a skier is in less than perfect balance.

When I first showed the above chart to a young downhill racer, she exclaimed with a laugh: "*That's* why I went in the woods off the Aspen bump! I was a tenth of a second late starting my turn—that's nine feet!"

chapter 14

Two Laws
from Newton

"*FOR EVERY ACTION THERE IS AN EQUAL AND OPPOSITE REACTION.*" This is the most interesting law of physics for snow skiers to contemplate. To understand it well, you have only to stand in the middle of your living room floor and try the following.

1. Bend forward at the waist without moving your hips back.
2. Bend your knees while keeping your back straight.
3. Bend your knees while keeping your back straight—and prohibiting your knees from moving forward.
4. Bend forward at the waist—allowing free movement of your body to maintain balance.

Please do these exercises and think about them before reading on. The figures in Drawing 21 illustrate the result of each movement.

Obviously Figures 1 and 3 are out of balance. Figure 2 has good balance. Figure 4, though in balance, suffers a loss of agility and strength because his back muscles are straining to support his "hanging upper body."

Each of these exercises illustrates that when any part of your body moves in one direction, another part must move in the opposite direction to maintain balance. There is obviously less movement of body mass in the action of Figure 2 than of Figure 4. Seeking economy of motion, therefore, it makes sense when bending the knees to press them forward.

Now look at the figures in Drawing 22.

Illustrated this way, it is obvious that just raising one arm will move your center of mass, or place you off balance. Is it a significant amount? Yes! If no body movement is made to compensate for the balance change, weight distribution will change on your skis, as in Figure 2. If your hip moves to maintain balance, the resulting angulation changes

(Drawing #21)

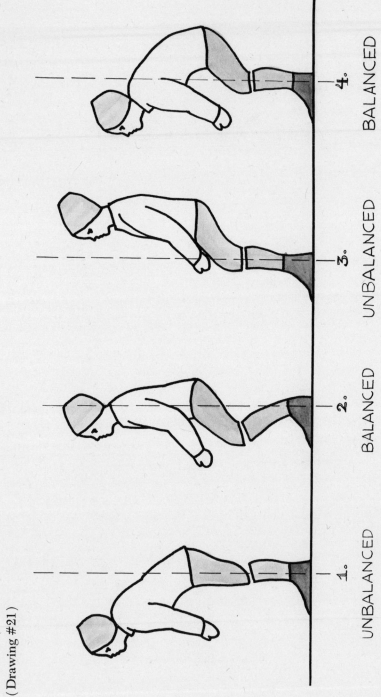

UNBALANCED   1.   BALANCED   2.   UNBALANCED   3.   BALANCED   4.

(Drawing #22)

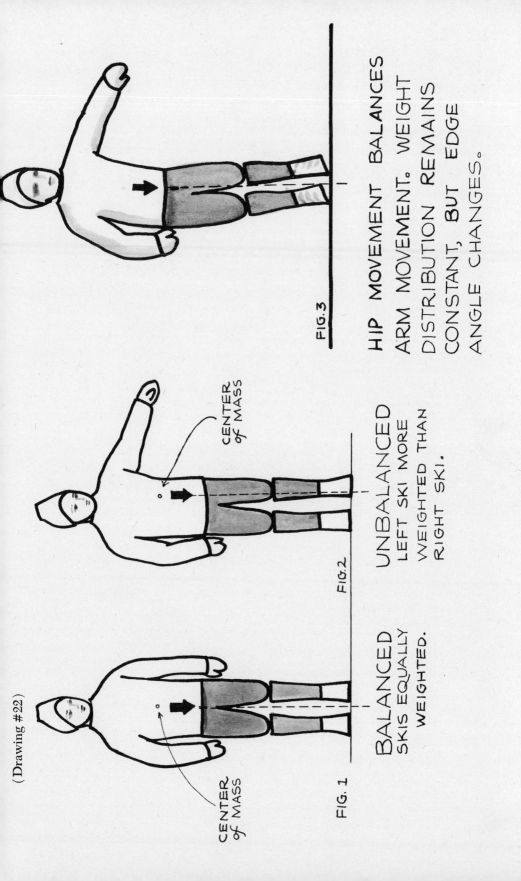

FIG. 1

BALANCED
SKIS EQUALLY
WEIGHTED.

CENTER
of MASS

FIG. 2

UNBALANCED
LEFT SKI MORE
WEIGHTED THAN
RIGHT SKI.

CENTER
of MASS

FIG. 3

HIP MOVEMENT BALANCES
ARM MOVEMENT. WEIGHT
DISTRIBUTION REMAINS
CONSTANT, BUT EDGE
ANGLE CHANGES.

the edge angle of your skis as in Figure 3. Either way, the turning action of your skis is affected.

Now think about your pole-plant action. How much does your arm move with each pole plant? Do you counterbalance this movement with your other arm? With your head? Or with your hips? Whatever your method, the body motion is undesirable.

In addition to requiring counterbalancing movements, all body motions create "momentum problems." Newton's applicable law is:

"A BODY IN MOTION WILL CONTINUE IN THE SAME DIRECTION AND AT THE SAME SPEED UNTIL ACTED UPON BY AN OUTSIDE FORCE." Every body movement, such as raising an arm, requires an additional muscle action to stop raising the arm. Excess motion is thus complicated at every step, and the case for disciplined body movement becomes increasingly strong. What are the results of simply raising one arm unnecessarily? The movement changes the pressure of your skis on the snow. As your arm is rising, pressure is increased. When you block the upward arm motion, pressure on the snow is decreased. *Each pressure change affects the carving action of your skis.*

There are times when you intentionally change the pressure on your skis by up or down body movements; but to have that pressure change at random as a result of unnecessary movements is hardly desirable. Precision control of your skis is sacrificed. That's why, in racing, the skier with the smoothest, most disciplined run often has the fastest time. The movement of an arm affects not only pressure, but also balance, and hence leverage and edge angle. Both affect the turning power of a ski. That is why, whenever possible, your hands or arms should move in mirror image, so one balances the movement of the other and balance of the main body mass is not disturbed. Look again at Photos 13A and 13B. Russell has the most disciplined hand and upper-body movements of any racer in the world.

There are almost endless applications of the above two laws of physics to all aspects of ski technique. I have pointed only to the most obvious. Thoughtful skiers, and particularly racers seeking a competitive edge, must evaluate all movements with an awareness of the secondary effects their movements create—especially the final effect on their skis' relationship to the snow.

chapter 15

On Sitting Back

The life of a ski coach is often devoted to fighting senseless habits and fads. One year racers are waving their arms wildly about; the next year they are bobbing their heads. The current rage is "sitting back." Unfortunately, skiing in a sitting-back position is not a local and short-term fad—it's a world-wide movement. It has been glorified by the ski press in words and pictures until recreational skiers as well as racers have been led to believe that turning on the back of their skis is the ultimate development of modern technique. It is not. It's a current fad, a new toy—and a promotional gimmick for selling ski magazines. Some perspective on sitting back is sorely needed in ski circles.

European technicians point to the Swiss racer Duveng Giavanoli as the pioneer of back-leverage turns. French and other coaches considered carefully the possibilities for acceleration that turning on the tail of the skis provided. They explored the potentials—and the best racers made *selective* use of back leverage. "Avalement" and "jet turns" gained world-wide publicity with Killy's racing successes in 1967 and 1968; and later with Patrick Russell, who has most perfectly mastered the art of carving turns with back leverage.

The skiing press has, unfortunately, printed pictures of Killy and Russell in low-hip, sitting-back, *off-balance* positions that are way out of proportion to the actual use of such a stance by these skiers. The fact is that both Killy and Russell skied with extraordinary discipline and balance—and speed. They occasionally got in trouble at the end of turns or between gates; and the press printed those pictures. They were exciting photos, but they did not show turns; they showed recoveries between turns. Killy and Russell won races by making 90 per cent of their turns in perfect balance. No one wins World Cup races without skiing a very precise line in almost perfect control. Like all great skiers, Killy and Russell made use of the whole ski, using forward, neutral, and back leverage to carve precise turns. When they used back leverage, it was a subtle distribution of pressure just behind the center of their skis; it seldom involved an extreme shift of body positions to a stance like that of a person sitting in a chair.

A study of recent films shows that Russell is highly selective in the situations where he employs extreme back leverage—only a few turns out of sixty in any given race. These are usually in gates with minimal direction change on slopes of moderate pitch. On steeper terrain, where there is room between gates to recover, some turns are ended with back leverage; but these turns are usually begun with forward leverage from an erect and balanced stance.

Gustavo Thoeni, the 1971 and '72 World Cup Champion, stands especially erect over his skis. He uses a consistently higher hip position than most other racers on the World Cup circuit. Fred Langendorf, director of Spalding's ski division, wrote to me in 1971: "The Sideral skis which Thoeni uses are not designed to make jet turns only, full well knowing that the sitting back position is a momentary thing in any turn, and standing over the skis is the backbone of any good skier."

The plain fact is that the world's best racers do not use a "sitting-back" technique as a basic way of skiing. The young French racers are making less use of back leverage than Russell. They are trying to ski in a position over the center of their skis which offers optimum balance and control. They are using forward leverage to initiate most turns in slalom, giant slalom, and downhill.

Both slalom and giant slalom courses have become increasingly fast in the past few years. The higher speeds in both events dictate greater requirements of balance and precise line, as opposed to needs for acceleration. The speeds at which the racers are traveling are conducive to initiating turns with forward leverage and a pure carving motion. In addition, the faster courses leave little time for racers to regain balance between turns. A consistently balanced position is required.

Significantly, the two best slalom skiers in the world today are Augert and Thoeni. Both ski in a consistently more erect position, and with greater use of forward leverage to initiate turns than most of their competitors on the World Cup circuit. Look again at Photo 13C, p. 76.

I do not wish to imply that it's always wrong to sit back—at the end or the beginning of turns. Sitting back is fun, and sometimes the fastest turns can be made by "carving on the tail." Good skiers should master all the design capabilities of their skis. "Sitting back," however, must be seen as a variation from basic technique, not as a natural

14. *Extreme forward leverage is applied by Augert to initiate this turn. Note the carving action of his ski tips. Such dynamic forward pressure is useful only at high speeds, and only for the initiation phase of a turn where the radius is shortening. As this turn progresses, Augert will adjust his leverage to near neutral for that period of the turn where a sustained arc is required. He may well finish the turn with back leverage, if there is room to recover to a neutral position before beginning his next turn. The adjustments of leverage depend on the position of the next gate, and the angle of turn it requires. Turns as sharp and as fast as that pictured here cannot be effectively initiated with neutral or back leverage. Carving on the front of the skis is required; and every single competitor in a World Cup field would use forward leverage to begin this turn.*

Photo
14

There are turns in most races that can be made with either forward or back leverage. Augert, when this judgment must be made, tends to use more forward pressure than most world class skiers. Russell will use back leverage in turns where Augert will not. The difference is determined by the skills each racer has; and those skills are at least in part determined by body build and muscle structure limitations. No other racer in the world has the physical capability to use back leverage as efficiently as Russell. Still, Russell begins almost all giant slalom turns with some forward leverage. It is the most efficient way to use the ski for high-speed turns that require a significant direction change, and that impose high centrifugal forces on the racer.

[103]

15. *Henri Duvillard, 1972 World Cup Runner-Up, attacks in slalom. This turn, made at a slower speed and requiring less direction change, demands less forward leverage than the turn by Augert shown on p. 103. Still, Duvillard exhibits the classic stance in the initiation phase of most slalom turns: erect upper body; hips balanced over or slightly ahead of the heels; forward drive of the knees. Note that Duvillard does not lean forward at the waist. To do so would require a backward movement of his hips to balance his body. The position of the knees and hips determines the leverage of the skier. The French are the best disciplined of the world's racers at maintaining an erect upper-body position. It is one of the keys to their continuing success in the Nation's Cup competition.*

MALCOLM REIS

16A and B. *Young American racers like Pete Murphy (top) and Chris Mike (bottom) are quickly developing the erect, attacking, stepping styles so efficiently used by racers like Thoeni, Duvillard, and Augert. Murphy, a Burke Mountain Racer, is the Eastern United States under-14 champion.*

16A

16B

stance. A low and back hip position does not satisfy the requirements for balance, strength, or economy of motion that an efficient ski technique demands.

Back leverage is used more often in soft snow than in hard. But even when free-skiing in soft snow, and carving turns "on the back of the ski," the aft leverage is subtle; an erect and balanced position is maintained about over the heel of your ski boot. That is a point only a few inches behind the center of a ski's running surface.*

Writing in *Ski* magazine ("Back Is Beautiful," February 1970). Joubert said: "The S turn is destined to become the advanced parallel form to which all good skiers will aspire in the 1970's." ("S turn" is Joubert's name for carved turns made with avalement from a consistently back position.) I take strong exception to this prediction. The S turn, like high fashion, is more stylish than necessary. Sound ski technique has been hampered by *style* for too many years. The body movements required by the "S turn" are much too extreme. They are as inefficient as Austrian reverse shoulder. Just as the comma position required too much twisting and bending, so does the "S turn" involve too much sitting back and bending.

So don't be swayed by French perfume. Remember that the S turn and all related sitting-back, avalement-oriented turns are variations on sound technique; they are not a foundation. The world's best skiers are standing over the middle of their skis—beginning turns with forward leverage, and often ending them with back leverage. Their back movements are, on the average, more subtle than their forward distribution of pressure. The important thing is that a balanced position over the center of the ski is "home base." All movements forward or back from center must be for the specific purposes of creating turning forces in the skis.

* It must be clear that "sitting back" (an extreme body position) and "using back leverage" (possible from a well-balanced stance) are two very different things. The skiing public, misled by countless magazine articles and photos, has failed to understand this important distinction.

part IV

Ski School

WEATHER STATION

SNOW TONITE

SKI MAINTENANCE

PHYSICAL TRAINING

PHYSICS LAB
SKI DESIGN   BODY MECHANICS

BOOK STORE

DON'T JUST SIT ON CHAIRLIFTS — READ

SKI SCHOOL   OPEN 8:00 A.M - 10:00 P.M.

WEDGES

SOLD HERE

MOVIE

THE SLALOM TURN with ANNEMARIE PROELL and GUSTAVO THOENI

chapter 16

A New Curriculum

The greatest need of ski schools is to think of themselves as *schools* —as places where uninformed people can really learn something.

What could people study in ski schools?

1. Ski design.
2. Body mechanics.
3. Equipment care (edge sharpening, bottom maintenance, etc.)
4. Balance: wedges and heel lifts.
5. Proper pole length and use.
6. Physical training.
7. Safety binding adjustment.
8. How a ski works: the result of edge, pressure, and leverage change.
9. Specific turns.

Each of the above subjects can be shown to increase the skiing ability of any recreational skier. Yet I can count on one hand the number of American ski schools that teach even two of these subjects on a regular basis. The major responsibility for educating the American public about skiing has been left to the skiing magazines and the periodical press. The ski schools should be ashamed!

At the Burke Mountain Alpine Training Center we teach all of these subjects. We use formal lectures. We use movies specifically designed to explore modern technique. We work individually with each "pupil" on the preparation and maintenance of his skis. We check the location and tension of his bindings. We check the pupil for wedges and heel lifts, and provide both as required.

I generally refuse to go on the hill with a pupil in my racing school until he has been checked for wedges, and properly supplied. If a racer needs wedges, and doesn't have them, he can't efficiently perform the technical maneuvers we strive to teach him and he wants to learn. All new pupils have their safety bindings checked before they ski. All new pupils during their first day attend a lecture on "ski mechanics, efficiency, race technique, etc."—they study a film on the "Fundamentals of Alpine Racing Technique." The film teaches all the basics covered in this book. Even Class A racers are asked to spend from one hour to half a day doing slow-speed maneuvers and snowplow turns in order to thoroughly understand how their skis work in the snow.

In summary, we *teach* skiing. We assume that even eight-year-olds can learn relevant ski mechanics, and can learn to prepare their equipment to perform to design potentials. They do, in fact, learn how their skis work in the snow, and they take meticulous care of them. They learn to ask "Why?" every time a coach tells them something. They study skiing, and they understand it.

Given half a chance, the American skiing public could be interested in the same subjects that fascinate young racers. Most ski-school pupils have as much desire to improve as the racers with whom I work. They only need to be offered a relevant curriculum, and to be inspired by good teachers.

It may be hard to teach the subjects suggested here during standard ski school hours: 10:00 to 12:00, and 1:00 to 3:00. At the Burke Training Center our normal coaching day runs from 8:30 to 4:30. We often teach until 6:00.

There are limits, of course, to how much material can be covered in one lesson. The majority of American ski-school pupils are now "Ski Weekers"—people on five- or seven-day vacation plans. If I ran a major ski school for these people, they would spend the first half day, and thereafter at least one hour per day, in the classroom: working on their equipment, studying films, *learning about skiing*.

The primary responsibility of a ski school is to help its customers progress as rapidly as possible. To assume this can be done with only on snow "do as I do" instruction is an incredibly unimaginative view. At Burke Mountain, instructors in the regular ski school (not the race training center) do four things for each student who enrolls.

1. They check his skis, making sure his edges are sharp and his bottoms are flat, etc.
2. They check his bindings to be certain they are properly adjusted for release, and will hold the skier's boots with maximum control.

3. They check his ski poles for proper length.
4. They check his need for wedges.

If poles are too long they shorten them (no charge). If wedges are needed, they provide them (at reasonable cost). If skis are in poor shape, they explain what needs to be done and either teach the customer to do it or send him to the ski school specialties shop where a full-time ski mechanic is employed to perform all aspects of ski maintenance. Thus the ski school assumes its proper responsibility—to assist each pupil in obtaining maximum efficiency from his equipment. Only then can the pupil's progress on snow proceed at an optimum pace.

By contrast, most ski schools accept the equipment limitations of their customers. This limits the progress each customer can make regardless of the caliber of on-snow instruction provided.

What we have done at the Burke Mountain Training Center represents only a few steps in the right direction. We have begun to look at ski teaching from a broad educational perspective. We have provided a complete equipment workshop. We have developed a film library catalogued for "fundamentals," "slalom," "giant slalom," and "downhill." For each event we combine films of world-class racers, and films of kids making the same mistakes as those we are coaching. We use videotape for same-day analysis of skier's techniques, and super 8 film for more detailed slow-motion analysis.

All good ski schools should have film libraries that explore the fundamental problems their pupils encounter at each stage of ski instruction. A stem-christie class meeting at 10:00 AM, should study a film on stem christies for twenty minutes before going on the hill. In a warm room with good acoustics, enormous teaching efficiencies could be achieved. The Professional Ski Instructors of America should prepare and distribute films of this kind for participating ski schools. Using just one projection room, two or three different levels of films could be shown each day between 9:00 and 10:00 AM.

If you're looking for a good ski school, forget the fancy European names and their "ex-junior champion" race records. What the ski-teaching profession needs is some *teachers*—educators who will respect the total learning ability of their pupils, and who can develop complete programs of instruction. To accomplish these goals, ski instructors must accept something more rigorous than their current four-hour workday (private lessons excluded). Time must be spent in the classroom, the workshop, the film lab, the videotape replay room, etc.

Instructors must assume a heavy responsibility for the equipment preparation of each person in their classes. This is the most important obligation ski schools have to their customers. It cannot be met between 10:00 and 12:00. Countless ski instructors have told me they can't teach the public the kind of techniques I teach my racers because the public's equipment is inadequate. That's humbug. Some ski pupils have poor equipment. Others have outstandingly good equipment—though usually it is poorly maintained. If their average pupil has inadequate equipment, or needs wedges, or needs to have his bindings properly located, or his edges sharpened—then the ski school should identify these needs, and satisfy them. That would be ski *teaching*. It would be helpful to break up classes in large ski schools to offer stem christie for students with good equipment, and stem christie for students with inadequate equipment. That would make people think about sharpening their edges! The "good equipment" group would be delighted; and the "inadequate equipment" group would at least feel they were getting special attention for their problems.

If a skier with dull edges came to my ski school for a week of instruction, and my mountain was hard ice, I would rather take a half day to fix his skis and give him a *half day's* instruction than leave his skis dull and give him a *week's instruction*. The one-day effort including equipment preparation would produce more results for the skier! It's a question of priorities.

The average American ski instructor has too limited an idea of his responsibilities—and of his opportunities. He doesn't teach half of what he knows; and he doesn't know all that he should. Significant changes in ski-school teaching will occur as instructors develop more faith in the capacity of their students to learn about skiing; and as instructors accept the full responsibilities of working in ski *school*. When the Professional Ski Instructors of America set their collective minds to schooling people as well as skiing with them—then they will begin to adequately serve the skiing public.

chapter 17

A Teaching System for Modern Race Technique

I cannot, in the scope of this book, outline a complete teaching program for all skiers from first-time beginners to advanced racers. The current teaching methods of most ski schools are well thought out as to sequence of maneuvers and useful exercises for the early stages of instruction. The same basic sequences are used by the Burke Mountain Ski School, only they teach carved turns from the very beginning—carved snowplow turns, and stem turns, and wide-track parallel. They teach a natural, balanced, square, comfortable stance for all maneuvers. They teach beginners, intermediates, and experts "how the ski works"; they teach skiers how to use their knees and ankles to change edge and pressure on their skis. They teach that the ski is a tool—that if you just stand on it properly, it will provide turning force. They teach people to "feel the snow." They teach people to edge their skis first, and then turn them. They stress that the upper body's main function is to maintain balance—that quiet, disciplined upper-body movements are essential to sound ski technique.

This whole approach to skiing is remarkably simple. Students at all levels of learning find it easy, efficient, and comfortable. It is, in a word, more *natural* than the Official American Ski Technique. Particularly, it requires that students spend less time doing formal "exercises," and more time skiing freely.

CARVED SNOWPLOW TURNS AND "JET PLOWS"

One aspect of teaching carved turns deserves special emphasis—the carved snowplow turn.

[113]

I use snowplow turns to teach racers the fundamentals of how a ski works in the snow: To teach them to feel the snow; to teach them to explore their ski's reactions to forward and backward leverage; to teach them the difference between carved and skidded turns; to teach them to work for maximum speed on a slow line; to teach them the secrets of accelerating their skis at the end of a turn; and to teach them how to make smooth transitions from a turning ski to a straight tracking traverse.

Yes—*all* these basic elements of skiing can be taught from snowplow turns. In fact, they are *best* taught from snowplow turns. Why? The snowplow position on a gentle slope is stable and secure. Turns can be made at very slow speeds, allowing a skier to concentrate on spe-

17. The author makes a snowplow turn steering with his left ski. He combines a skidding of the ski with the maximum carving potential afforded by the ski design for a turn of this radius and speed. Note the reverse camber in the edged and weighted left ski. The right ski is lightly weighted and is used only for balance. Note the similarity between the author's stance in this picture and in Photo 10. The following picture shows the track left in the snow by this turn. The author's left ski made the track furthest to the right in the photograph. The center track is from another skier. The track on the left is that of the author's lightly weighted uphill ski.

MALCOLM REISS

MALCOLM REISS

18. *This picture shows clearly the transition from steered turn to a purely carved traverse. The end of the turn and the traverse are made without any skidding of the ski. Note the similarity between this track and that left by Mike Raymaley's slalom turn in Photos 9A and 9B. The track of the author's inside ski deserves attention. A right turn is made on the left edge; and there is no evident skidding of the ski. The racer's instinct to eliminate all braking actions is demonstrated here. How is this done? Can you find the answer by studying Photo 17?*

cific details—to isolate each factor of a turn and to think analytically about it.

When coaching new students, I take them to an easy slope and ask them to do a series of snowplow turns. After watching ten snowplow turns, I can identify almost every problem each racer will have in fast parallel skiing, or in running slalom gates. What do I see?

First, I study each skier's control of his skis. Does he steer and carve precise turns, or does he skid? Are his turns made on a smooth arc or a varied arc? I learn by these observations how precise his edge control is—and how well he uses his skis to create turning forces. (See Photos 17 and 18.)

Second, I study each skier's body positions. How much upper-body rotation does he use to make each turn? Does he hold his hands quietly and always in front of his body? If so he will do the same in slalom. If he rotates his shoulders in the direction of each snowplow turn, he will do the same in parallel turns. If he leans inside each turn with his head, he will do the same in giant slalom. Every aspect of a skier's stance and balance, and the use he makes of his body in each turn, is evident in linked snowplow turns.

I discuss unnecessary and inefficient motions with each skier. I teach him to make snowplow turns without upper-body rotation. "Just stand in perfect balance on your skis," I say. "Press your knees forward to increase leverage and inside to roll your ski on edge." The wide stance of a snowplow position provides continual hip angulation in relation to the outside ski. (See Photo 17.) At slow speed—where he has maximum control, confidence, and concentration—a racer can learn to make his skis carve by just standing on them properly.

We do snowplow turns for miles! We learn to "feel the snow," to feel the tip of the ski lead the turn—carving, biting. We learn to make turns of a perfectly smooth arc by maintaining constant pressure and edge on the ski. We learn the difference between jamming turns (pushing too hard on the ski) and applying pressure smoothly. We learn to initiate turns with a pure carving motion—or in many slow turns—to use steering at the start of the turn, and then finish the turn with a carving action of the ski. (See Photo 18.) We stop frequently to examine the tracks we leave in the snow, learning from them how skidded and carved turns vary in arc and resistance. We work (at 3 to 5 MPH) to create acceleration from our skis—to push the skis ahead of our center of gravity as the turn progresses so pressure distribution moves toward the tail. We experiment with 10 or 20 or 30 degrees of edge angle. We explore how much edge is required to carve each turn without skidding. We try making turns with forward, neutral, and aft leverage; we discover the full range of ski responses to each input of edge angle and pressure.

The final goal of these snowplow turns is to do "jet plows"—snowplow turns with a noticeable acceleration at the end of the turn. The challenge, as in all racing turns, is to lock the ski on edge in a straight traverse at the instant the ski is heading in the direction the racer desires to go—i.e., if a racer is turning from south to west, in the exact instant his ski comes around the arc to the west heading, he must lock that ski on edge (no sideslip) and accelerate it straight toward the starting point of the next turn. In snowplow maneuvers racers can learn to feel each sensitive step in ski control that produces maximum acceleration.

After they develop the ability to make good "jet plow turns," I ask skiers to do a series of snowplow turns linked by short traverses—first trying to create maximum speed in four successive turns, then doing four skidded ski-school turns (weight on heel of ski, heel thrust, "bowing over the outside ski," etc.) These skidded snowplow turns create an incredible braking effect. They reduce a skier's speed by as much as 50 per cent. Then four more carved snowplow turns build up the speed again, and four skidded turns reduce it. There is no exercise that more clearly demonstrates to any racer—class A or D—the significance of carving turns. After first doing this exercise, kids have an absolutely incredulous look on their faces. They can't believe the speed differential. I simply say: "Now you understand why you are ten seconds behind world-class skiers on a sixty-second course!" They understand how important carved turns are—and they understand how to make them.

Skeptics may claim this whole exercise is unreal—that snowplow turns are done on one ski, that the racer never has to change edge while in the snowplow position. So be it. It's important to be comfortable on one ski; and racing technique requires an almost continual shifting of weight from one ski to the other. The simplicity of snowplow maneuvers makes it possible for each youngster to fully understand how his skis work. *That knowledge is a prerequisite for all other learning about racing technique.*

In short, every fundamental concept of efficient ski-racing technique, except edge change, can be taught doing snowplow maneuvers. An equivalent understanding can never be gained from high-speed skiing, as too many separate things happen too fast for the racer to feel them individually, and to understand their relationship to one another. Whether you are teaching beginner or expert, using GLM (Graduated Length Method) or full-length skis, the snowplow turn is a testing laboratory where at slow speed, and in perfect control, every aspect of turning skis can be explained, explored, and discovered.

Whenever we teach new concepts to a racer, we begin on easy terrain. This is an important point for any ski-teaching system. New skills are most quickly acquired under easy learning conditions. If you try to teach people to carve turns on difficult and steep terrain, they will have great difficulty. They must learn on smooth, flat slopes where they can let their skis run, where balance is easy, where without fear of speed they can concentrate on feeling their skis work for them. After acquiring new skills, and perfecting them on easy terrain, then the skills can be applied to more difficult trails.

Photo
19

MALCOLM REISS

19. *Mary Beth Quinn, a 14-year-old Burke skier, explores ways to accelerate her ski at the end of a jet plow turn. Mary Beth is applying pressure to her left ski at the same time she pushes her foot forward. This will help the ski end the turn with a carving motion. The edge-set achieved here will provide a platform for shifting her weight to the right ski for the following turn.*

In this exercise, Mary Beth is learning to use the full design potential of her skis at two critical parts of a racing turn: 1) the transition from a skidding to a carving ski in steered turns, and 2) the art of neutralizing a turn so her ski accelerates on a straight traverse path. These skills, learned in slow motion, can be quickly applied to faster turns under racing conditions. The whole art of feeling the snow is best learned at snowplow speeds.

part V Equipment

Without attention to the subject matter of the three chapters in this part, all technical progress in skiing is seriously limited. Superb equipment care is a prerequisite to maximum enjoyment of the sport of snow skiing.

chapter 18

Preparation and Care of Your Skis

SKIS FUNCTION PROPERLY ONLY WHEN THEY ARE PERFECTLY "TUNED." It is impossible to ski well with dull edges, excessively convex or concave bottoms, improperly placed bindings, and the like.

Nearly all recreational skiers, and most developing racers too, greatly handicap their technical progress and limit their enjoyment of snow skiing because they are too lazy or too ignorant to properly prepare and maintain their equipment. Most skiers treat their skis like their automobiles—they take them to the shop for service every six thousand miles. That may suffice for Mom's Ford, but racing machines require more attention. If you would ski as the best racers do, you must prepare your skis as they do. No youngster whom I coach would consider skiing on a *new* pair of skis until he had spent the better part of an hour preparing the bottoms and edges.

PREPARATION OF NEW SKIS

I don't know of any snow skis available today that are ready to be skied on as delivered by a retail shop. Nor do I know of any manufacturer or retail shop that publicly admits this to the ski purchaser. Keeping this secret has greatly reduced the pleasures people can derive from skiing.

Due to problems in mass production, the edges and bottoms of all skis are smoothed on some kind of belt or drum sander. Two problems result that seriously affect a ski's performance. First, the bottoms are convex. The softer P-Tex running surface is displaced more quickly by the sander than are the steel rails on the sides of the ski. The result, when the ski is turned bottom up as in Drawing 23 is that the edges are "high." The ski base is concave. This causes the ski to perform as though it were riding on rails—the edges—rather than on the

[121]

(Drawing #23)

entire base. This concavity causes the ski to "hook" or to turn in jerky movements. Smooth transitions from one edge to the other are difficult.

Ski bottoms should be perfectly flat. Some will perform adequately when slightly concave; but this concavity must be in the inner portion of the ski. The edges must be flat for at least one-half inch in from the edge. (See Drawing 24.)

Bottoms are most easily filed with a ten-inch mill bastard file. For bottom-filing, most people prefer to pull the file rather than push it. It is helpful to secure your skis on a bench as illustrated. Use blocks to raise the skis until the bindings are clear of the table. A vise or fixed stop will prevent the skis from sliding.

Note that the teeth on a file are slanted. The file only cuts in the direction the teeth "bite." Thus, to have the file cut when you pull it, you must hold the handle in your left hand. When pushing the file, you must hold the handle in your right hand. By trial and error you will find the file cuts best at an angle not quite perpendicular to the ski edge. (See Photos 20A and B.)

THESE AREAS MUST BE PERFECTLY FLAT.

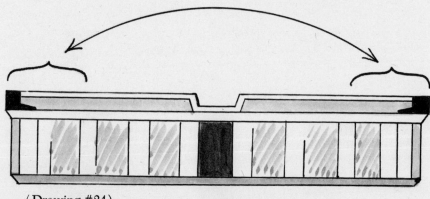

(Drawing #24)

20A. *Pulling the file. The handle must be held in the left hand. Thumb pressure is over the edges.*

20B. Pushing the file. The handle must be held in the right hand. Pressure is applied over the edges by the index fingers.

When you begin filing new skis you can feel and hear the file cutting only the steel edges. As the edges are filed down to the level of the P-Tex base, the file will slide more smoothly and more quietly. It will begin to pick up P-Tex shavings the color of the ski base; the base will appear shiny next to the edge where the file has smoothed it. Continue flat-filing until this shine extends at least one-half inch inward from both edges. At this point the bottom is sufficiently flat to ski well. Be sure to hold the file flat on your skis. A ten-inch file will bend if you press on the ends. To keep the file flat, pressure should be applied with the thumbs directly over the steel edges.

As you file, you will notice that the teeth of the file draw steel shavings from one edge onto the P-Tex. Continually brush these shavings away so as not to grind them into the base. Shavings from the other edge will drop off beside the ski. For the best possible job, concentrate your pressure on the edge that files clean. Then switch directions with the file. This way you finish each edge by drawing the shavings off the ski.

You may flat-file from tip to tail or from tail to tip. It is possible to do this job with the ski standing against a wall or leaning on a chair, but the most precise work can be done on a stable bench with the ski firmly fastened. As you file, continually brush the steel and P-Tex accumulations from the file teeth. Use a "file card" or wire brush to do this job.

Photo
20B

To persons who seldom use tools, or who have had little experience with a file, this operation may at first seem awkward. A file, however, is a simple tool; with a little practice you can develop a good feel for it. I work with racers, boys and girls, less than ten years old who are excellent at filing skis. Racers should always file their own skis so their bottoms and edges will at all times be identically prepared.

As girls' hands are less strong than boys, it is especially important that girls work wih sharp files. They cut more precisely and with less effort. Dull files only rub on metal; they don't cut it. Serious skiers should buy eight- and 10-inch files by the dozen. (They make useful Christmas presents, and most hardware stores will give discounts for volume purchases.) I always use a new file to prepare new skis, or to work on old skis that require an equivalent amount of edge be removed. Once skis are in perfect tune, a file will last for a week of daily touch-ups. When a file becomes dull, throw it away.

It is important that you get the bottom of all new skis absolutely flat within the tolerances stated above. Despite the experiences I have had preparing hundreds of new snow skis, I occasionally think I have properly filed a ski only to find that the ski still "hooks"—i.e., it does not turn smoothly or maintain a constant radius of turn under constant pressure. This is a sure sign that some part of the ski base is not properly flat-filed. Sometimes two or three light passes over just a few inches of one edge will completely cure the problem—perhaps the shaving of one or two thousandths of an inch!

After the ski base is prepared, a hand-filing of the edges (sides) is also required. In the final steps of manufacture, most skis are passed across a drum sander to "finish" the edges. The skis are held by hand and moved back and forth across the drum. No worker is so skilled he can hold the ski at a constant angle to the drum; nor can he maintain equal pressure all along the edge. Waves result in the edge, especially near the tip and tail where the worker is reaching at full arm's length.

To sharpen the sides of the skis, it is best to place the ski on edge and secure it in a vise. If a vise is not available, wedge the ski into a corner, or against a door jamb. Hold the ski against or between your legs so it rocks as little as possible.

There are two basic methods of edge sharpening. The first is to hold the file in two hands and draw or push it just as you do when bottom-filing. For girls and for children with weak hands this often works best. One must be careful not to tilt the file and produce an "off-square" edge. Most people with stronger hands and a good feel for tools prefer to hold the file in one hand and push it along the edges as shown in Photos 21A and B.

A file cuts most efficiently in this direction, and with practice the best edge is thus obtained. As with bottom-filing, you must keep the teeth clean as you work. A square edge is desired. Be careful not to tilt your file as you work. An eight-inch file is preferable for edge-filing. It is lighter, more easily controlled with one hand; and it has finer teeth than a ten-inch file. Some racers use six-inch files for very light finish work.

Edge-file only until 1) the entire side of your ski edge is smooth (no waves or ripples), and 2) there is a clean 270-degree corner at all points along the edge. A "clean corner" assures maximum sharpness as both side and bottom edges display clean steel—just filed. The clean steel will shine under direct light. As in sharpening a knife, you must sharpen to the very edge of the blade.

Only after these filing operations are complete is a new pair of skis ready to perform according to its design potential.

After filing your skis, you should wax them to seal the P-Tex base and to provide a faster running surface. Wax should be applied with a warm iron. If the iron is too hot, it will affect the glue bond between the P-Tex and the ski core. Be careful never to let the iron rest in one place on the ski. Move the iron quickly along the ski base.

There are many methods of wax application, from dripping the wax off an iron to melting it in a pot and brushing it on. I prefer a method taught me by a ten-year-old who had done some independent thinking. Place a warm iron beside your skis. Touch a bar of wax to the iron just long enough to soften the wax—then rub the soft wax quickly on the ski base. Three or four contacts of wax to iron will provide enough softened wax to rub a covering coat on the entire ski base. A little practice will teach you exactly how thick a coat is needed to cover the base so the iron will slide over the ski on a constant film of wax. Use as little wax as possible while still covering the ski. This saves wax and simplifies scraping.

A few quick passes over the ski with the iron will melt the wax so it soaks into and bonds well with the P-Tex base. Excess wax should then be scraped off with a stainless-steel cabinet scraper. Clean the groove with a coin or spoon. A smooth, thin coat of wax will be left on the ski base. It is important to file skis first, then wax them. If you wax first, the wax will clog the file teeth and make filing very difficult.

When your new skis are properly flat-filed, edge-filed, and waxed, then they are ready to work for you as they were designed to do.

MAINTAINING YOUR SKIS

Once you have prepared new skis (or rehabilitated old ones), it is imperative that you keep them in "racing tune." The easiest way to do this is with a light touch-up *every day*.

When you finish skiing, stand your skis against a wall or table (bottoms up) and very lightly take a smooth stroke along the whole base. This stroke is not to file the bottoms, but to feel for burrs on the edges. If you have hit no rocks or other obstacles, the base should feel flat and smooth, except in the shovel area. At the widest part of the shovel, where your inside edges bang together, there will be a small burr on the bottom edge. File this burr off every day. If there are other rough spots on your edges that have been caused by striking rocks, etc., file just these rough spots until they are smooth. No other bottom-filing should be necessary on a daily basis.

After making your bottoms flat and smooth, then edge-file until a smooth, sharp edge results. Be careful to take off only as much steel as you need to get a clean edge. If you sharpen your skis every day they are used, they will require only a light filing. Less than five minutes' work is involved. If you let your skis go for five days between filings, you will have five times as much steel to remove before you get

21A and B. Filing the edge—both left- and right-handed.

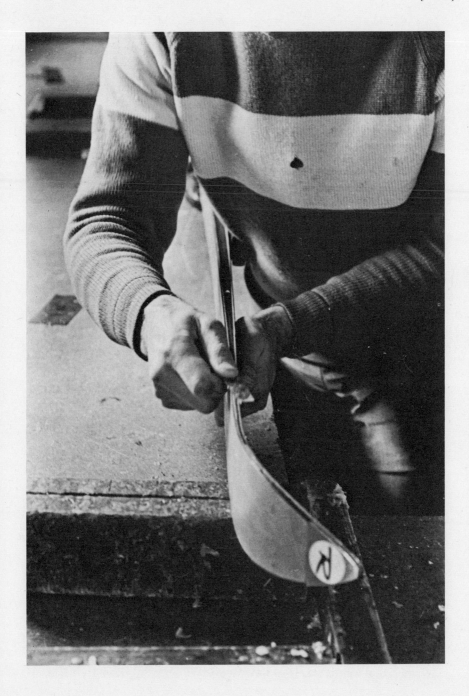

a clean, sharp edge. It is easier to sharpen a little bit every day. (It's like keeping a straight razor sharp—a couple of whomps on the strap every time you shave keeps it just right, but if you let the razor dull for a week, it's difficult to get a good edge again.)

Racers should finish their edges with a fine abrasive stone to remove the microscopic burrs left by the file. This step is unnecessary for recreational skiers.

Edges can be side-filed only until the steel edge is flush with the sidewall of the skis. Thus, it is important not to file edges more than is necessary to keep them sharp. Some high-priced skis have almost no offset edge. They should not be purchased. When buying skis remember that the useful life of the ski is determined by the amount of edge available to be sharpened.

As ski bottoms become gouged and edges are seriously burred, it is occasionally necessary to remove substantial amounts of bottom edge and P-Tex base to maintain a flat and smooth running surface. Perform this operation when required; but don't bottom-file your skis any more than necessary. The P-Tex base is quite thin, and can be planed off only a limited number of times.

In an effort to smooth bottom edges without thinning the P-Tex, many people gradually produce a convex bottom. This results from pressing on the ends of the file. As skis become too convex they ski with less precision. It is then necessary to flatten the bottoms by planing the P-Tex down to the level of the edges. This is best done with a sharp cabinet scraper.

This is a difficult job. Most skiers will have to ask a ski-repair shop to flatten convex bottoms with a belt sander. If you have skis with badly gouged bottoms and edges it may also be helpful to have the bottoms reconditioned on a ski-shop sander.

Warning: Many ski shops offer "edge sharpening" and "bottom reconditioning" services for prices ranging from $2.00 to $10.00. Most of these services are performed with belt or drum sanders. *They leave the skis with the same concave bottoms as new skis*—or because the ski-shop equipment is less sophisticated than factory sanders, with *worse* concavity. Thus, your ski shop may sharpen your edges and smooth your bottoms, but they will not tune your skis. A sander will do the rough work for you. You must follow up with a hand file to assure proper performance from your skis.

Perhaps as much damage is done to ski edges during car-top travel as on ski slopes. Car-top racks expose skis to damaging salt-water spray on most winter highways. The salt corrodes edges, and the water rusts them. Your bindings suffer too. Whenever possible, travel with your skis inside your car, or purchase a protective ski bag to cover your skis during transit. Most ski shops sell these bags at reasonable prices.

22. To plane P-tex bottoms, hold the scraper blade at the angle shown. Bend the blade slightly so as to plane only half the ski width at a time. With practice, P-tex shavings as large as those pictured here can be removed easily.

This chapter is long because of its instructional nature, but please don't think ski maintenance is difficult. You have only three things to do: Keep your ski bottoms flat; keep your edges sharp; and keep some wax in your P-Tex base. With a little practice the required skills can be mastered. You should then enjoy maintaining your skis. There is pleasure in working with tools; and you will develop sources of pride in producing a sharp edge. Most important, your skiing will improve if your skis are always tuned up. Good racers can ski with incredible precision on very hard ice. Their technique helps, of course; but one secret of their control is in the work they have done on their skis. Soft snow forgives many deficiencies in ski preparation. Hard snow exaggerates every flaw. It is not possible to ski well on hard snow unless your skis are in perfect racing tune.

Photo
22

chapter 19

Mounting Bindings

In order for skis to function properly, a skier's boots must be correctly located on his skis. A half-inch error in binding placement seriously impairs a ski's performance. For the accomplished racer, movement of one-eighth inch in binding placement noticeably changes the performance of a ski.

Many formulas have been devised for binding placement. All of them come close to placing the ball of the foot at the center of the running surface. As it is difficult to exactly measure the running surface, the following formula has been devised to accomplish this purpose.

For:	Place the toe of the boot:
Slalom skis	1 cm. (⅜″) ahead of chord length center*
Giant slalom skis	On chord length center
Downhill skis	I cm. (⅜″) behind chord length center

* Chord length is the straight line measurement from tail to tip. Do not measure around the bend in the tip.

(Drawing #25)

(Line with arrow is chord length)

These measurements are for boots size 8 to 10. For size 7 and under move the boot back one-eighth inch per whole size. For boots 11 and larger, move forward one-eighth inch per whole size.

Most people assume that slalom skis are mounted farther forward to put more pressure on the tip for quick turns, and that downhill skis are mounted further back for speed. This is not true. On all kinds of skis the boot placement is approximately the same in relation to the skis' running surface. Slalom skis have short tips, so the center of the running surface is relatively forward compared to downhill skis which have long tips.

To mount bindings, or to check the placement of bindings already mounted:

1. Measure the chord length of your ski.
2. Measuring from the tail, mark the ski at one-half the chord length. Adjust forward or back of this line for your boot size and type of ski.

If you have the proper tools, there is no reason you can't mount your own bindings. Most racers do. Mounting your bindings saves money (which can be invested in higher quality bindings) and assures that your bindings will be properly placed.

Care must be taken to mount bindings parallel to and on the center line of your skis. Most ski shops use factory-supplied jigs to accurately mark binding holes. Many ski shops will mark holes for you, and let you take your skis home to drill and screw. This saves time for harried shop owners who have trouble keeping up with their shop work.

If you don't know how to properly fit and adjust your bindings, you should, for safety's sake, have a reputable ski shop do that for you. If you leave your skis to be mounted by a shopman, be sure he knows exactly where you want the toe of your boot located. Measure and mark the skis yourself, then ask the shop to mount your bindings "with the toe of the boot on the scratch line."

Some manufacturers, such as Rossignol, put a decal on their skis to indicate proper boot location. ALL SKI MANUFACTURERS SHOULD DO THIS. IT IS IN THEIR OWN INTEREST TO ASSURE THAT ALL PURCHASERS GAIN MAXIMUM SATISFACTION FROM USE OF THEIR SKIS. Ski Industries of America should design a simple decal like Drawing 26 (next page). and request all ski manufacturers to properly position the decal on their skis.

As new developments occur in ski design, binding placement may vary considerably. The formula given at the beginning of this chapter is a broad compromise for most skis. Manufacturers should provide the

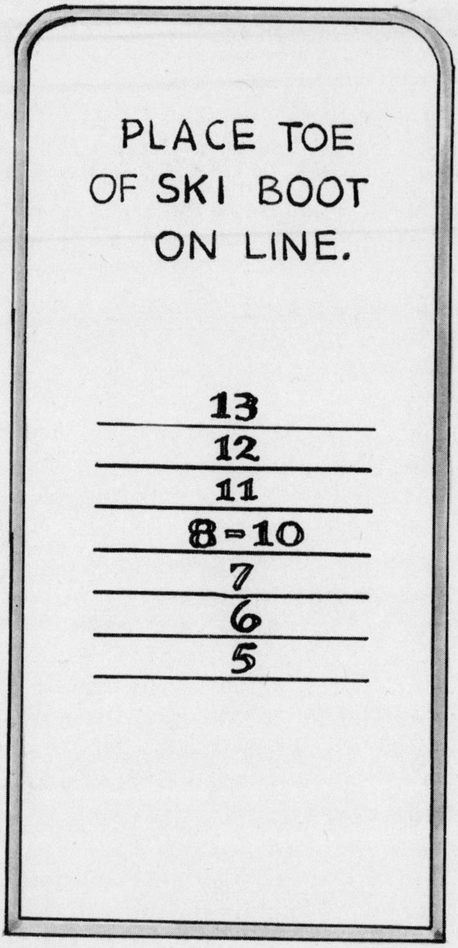

PLACE TOE
OF SKI BOOT
ON LINE.

(Drawing #26)

13
12
11
8-10
7
6
5

specific guides required to assure maximum performance of their products.

For your own safety, you should learn as much as you can about the design and function of your bindings. You should learn to adjust them for proper release, and for maximum control. Release settings should be checked every day you ski! Though you may not have daily access to a mechanical device such as the Lipe Release Check, you can check toe-piece settings by opening the units with thumb and forefinger pressure. Major errors in binding tension can easily be recognized in this way. If a binding is mechanically frozen, you will discover the danger. No binding should be used on a tighter setting than can be

opened by the hand of its user. To check heel-release units, have someone stand on the tails of your skis while you jam your knee forward
to provide heel lift. You should, with maximum effort, be able to step
out of your bindings.

It. is also imperative that you check each day to be certain your
boot is held as firmly to the ski as possible (without limiting the release capability of the binding). Most toe units should allow one-
thirty-second-inch play between the boot and the binding. This insures
the boot will not be jammed against the ski prohibiting lateral release.
Some bindings vibrate out of adjustment and require frequent tightening of the boot holding unit. As boot soles wear and warp, minor adjustments must be made to accommodate each change in the sole shape.

Many pages could be written here about specific care, adjustment,
and maintainance of the most popular ski bindings. Gordon Lipe has
done notable research and reporting in this area. I recommend that all
readers familiarize themselves with Mr. Lipe's work. He has published
frequently in Skiing magazine and in other ski industry journals.

One general point often stressed by Mr. Lipe is that an antifriction
plate should be mounted under the ball of the foot with almost all
safety toe units. This device not only improves the release efficiency
of the binding; it also places the ball of the foot in direct contact with
the ski. Most modern boots have such rigid soles that when the heel
is raised on a binding platform, the only forward part of the boot in
contact with the ski is the front edge of the sole. An antifriction plate
should be used that raises the front edge of the boot sole at least a
sixteenth of an inch off the ski. This improves efficiency of heel release
units, and provides ski contact under the ball of your foot.

chapter 20

Selecting Equipment

The carved-turn techniques of racers are possible *to a degree* on poor equipment; but if you want to reap the maximum enjoyment which skiing can offer, then you need the very best skis and boots. Sleep in a bag in a bunkhouse; ski in blue jeans and barn jackets if you must; but spend your hard-earned money on the tools you need. I have no sympathy for snow bunnies who have second-rate skis and high-class fashions in parkas, pants, and hats. If fashion is your bag, go dancing. If skiing is your thing, make every possible effort to acquire the best skis, boots, and bindings you can. They are more responsive and precise.

SKIS

If you're an expert skier, stick to the skis used by a large number of international-class racers—and to models that can be bought similar to those the racers use. If you're an intermediate skier, consider the models designed for your kind of skiing by the same manufacturers. They have the most ski-design and manufacturing experience.

Buy skis that have a proven record of satisfied users. Don't gamble on manufacturers who are trying to catch up. Be skeptical of "hot new products." It usually takes at least a year to get the bugs out of any new design, and to manufacture it with good quality control. Don't be swayed by cosmetics on the ski, by clever advertising, or by the propaganda of retail salesmen who have overstocked brands to push out of inventory.

Once you limit yourself to the very best brands, your problem is what length and model of ski to choose, and how to select a good pair.

Let's consider the model first: slalom, giant slalom, or downhill. Eliminate the downhill ski. It's a specially designed tool for high-speed racing (50 to 75 MPH). The skis are too heavy and unresponsive for pleasurable skiing at recreational speeds.

The choice of a slalom or giant slalom ski depends mostly on the type and speed of skiing you prefer. If you ski fast, and like to execute long turns, giant slalom skis are preferable. If you prefer to ski at slow or medium speeds, and you especially enjoy quick, precise turns, then slalom skis are best.

Skis like the Rossignol Strato 102 and the K2 Four are made almost identically for slalom and giant slalom. They are stable in long, fast turns and they are precise in shorter turns. For the faster event (giant slalom) racers choose a longer size of the same model they use for slalom. Young racers and recreational skiers who wish to invest in only one pair of skis are advised to select a length suitable for slalom. It will provide sufficient stability for skiing at giant slalom speeds; by contrast, an ideal giant slalom length will be too cumbersome for slalom.

If you're a rank beginner, rent good equipment while you are trying out the sport. Many ski schools now offer Graduated Length Method teaching for beginners. This means you start on small skis, which are especially easy to maneuver. I support this approach. The best GLM skis carve turns quite well. You can learn to ski as the racers do right from the start.

When you buy skis, even if you're a beginner, buy good ones! You'll learn faster on them. If your budget is limited, buy used top-of-the-line equipment. Good second-hand skis can be bought for $50 to $100 that will outperform equivalently priced new skis. If you have old dogs for skis, and slippers for boots, you can *never* learn to ski well. Don't waste two years on crummy equipment. Life is too precious.

How Long a Ski Should You Buy? Generally you should use skis two to eight inches longer than your height. Adjust in that range according to your weight and strength, and the speed at which you ski. A boy 5'8" weighing 150 pounds is often stronger than a six-footer of the same weight. There is no reason why the taller boy should ski on a longer ski. The following table is a general guide for ski selection. For slalom, or slow-speed recreation skiing, favor the short side of suggested lengths. For giant slalom or high-speed recreation skiing, tend toward the longer skis in each weight category.

Weight:	Ski Length:
100-110 lbs.	180-190cm
110-125	190-195
125-140	195-200
140-165	200-207
165-180	203-210
180-200	207-215

Children under one hundred pounds should not use skis longer than their height unless they are technically proficient; then two to four inches above their height will suffice. Adults who are old, slow, out of shape, or timid should select a size shorter than is listed in the chart. Gifted athletes who like to ski fast can select a ski one size larger than the standard recommendations.

How Do You Select Skis off the Rack? There are great variations in even the best skis. Stiffness, camber, and flex patterns all vary. When comparing different pairs of the same size and model you should:

1. Place the skis bottom to bottom. Be sure the camber is at least ¾″ and less than 1¼″.
2. Squeeze the skis together and check that the bottoms make contact along the entire running surface. If there are gaps between the skis, one or both skis must have an irregular flex pattern. When you squeeze the skis together at the waist, be sure the tips don't open excessively; i.e., the running surfaces must maintain contact in the shovel area. The tips should open *slightly* as you squeeze the ski's together, but this opening should not extend more than one-half inch along the running surface.
3. Clamping the skis together, be sure they are of equal width at all points. This assures you the side-cut of both skis is identical.
4. Check the edges to be sure there is sufficient off-set edge at all points. Especially check the shovel area.

Reject Skis That Fail Any of These Tests. From the skis not rejected for major flaws, select the softer pairs; they will turn more easily. Then select the pair with the best *flex pattern*. Check flex pattern as in Drawing 27.
When a ski is perfectly flat, there should be no "waves" in the edge line. When bent into reverse camber, the edge line should form a smooth arc. Flat spots in the flex arc detract from a ski's ability to carve precise turns.

When you have selected and purchased a good pair of skis, remember that you still have to hand-file the bottoms and edges to achieve the performance for which the skis are designed.

BINDINGS

Do not purchase or use low-cost release bindings. Broken legs are expensive and uncomfortable. Low-cost bindings are cheap because

(Drawing #27)

they are poorly engineered and are made of low-grade materials. Release bindings are a form of insurance. If you have to skip lunch for a week to afford them, buy the best bindings available.

About 90 per cent of the top-flight racers in the world use just three kinds of bindings. Their example should be followed. Reputable ski-shop owners or instructors can tell you at any given time what bindings are in use by international competitors. Follow their example and you will be assured of a superior product. As new developments come on the market, racers will be the first to test them. If they approve a binding and use it in competition, you can be certain it provides maximum control and safety.

POLES

Poles should be from 70 to 75 per cent of your height. If you are short, near 70 per cent. If you are tall, closer to 75 per cent. Final determination of length depends on various factors of a racer's technique and stance. A rule of thumb is that your forearm should be horizontal if you hold the pole normally by the grip and place the point on a hard floor. This should be done standing erect in ski boots.

If poles are too long, excessive lifting of your arms is required for each pole plant. This disturbs the maintenance of a quiet upper-body position. If poles are too short, you have to duck your shoulder or upper body to reach the snow for each pole plant. Again, undesirable body movements are caused.

You should purchase the lightest-weight poles you can afford. Swing weight and balance are as important as dead weight. Select a grip that is comfortable in your hands, and that has adjustable wrist straps. Adjustable straps allow you to wear different weight gloves or mittens, and to tighten the straps as they stretch with use. Always have the wrist strap tight when your hand is in its normal position on the pole grip. A tight strap greatly improves your pole control, and thus the precision with which you can ski.

So far, no manuafcturer has been able to produce a pole basket that is ultralight and really durable. Some are better than others. Baskets that break, or simply slip off the pole, are a continuing nuisance. When you buy poles, buy three or four extra baskets. Keep one in your car, and one in your ski kit. Then when you lose or a break a basket you'll have a replacement handy. Racers should keep a spare basket in their parka pocket on race days, so that last-minute breakage won't leave them ill-equipped in the starting gate.

GLOVES AND MITTENS

There are many fancy gloves and mittens available at prices up to $40.00. They have foam linings, and silver shields, and sub-zero guarantees. To the best of my knowledge, none of these "marvels of modern industry" are as warm as "fake fur"—alpaca pile linings. Alpaca pile comes in a variety of colors and costs about $16.00 in gloves and $12.00 in mittens. You can't beat it at any price.

On cold days, mittens are warmer than gloves. Don't be embarrassed to wear them.

BOOTS

It is difficult to write about specific boot models. There are too many, and designs are changing so fast that my comments would be out of date before this book is in print. The most important thing is to get a good fit. You can't ski well if your feet aren't comfortable. Unless you have a very standard foot, foam liners will usually improve fit, comfort, and control in any boot model.

The following guidelines may also be useful:

1. Buy plastic or synthetic boots. They wear longer than leather and they don't stretch when wet.

2. Buy the highest and stiffest boot that is comfortable for you, and is within your price range. But remember, some boots are too high and too stiff.

3. Avoid boots with excessive dials, springs, screws, and other gimmicks. In general the best boots are fairly simple in design. Be sure buckles and other hardware are strong, and that parts are available.

4. Other factors being equal, select the lightest boot available that provides adequate strength and durability.

5. As with bindings and skis, it is best to purchase those brands in common use by the best racers. You may wish a cheaper model than the Class A racer's boot, but the same manufacturers that are providing the favored racing boots also have the most experience and know-how in producing recreational boots.

Unless there is a good boot between you and your skis, precise control of your skis is impossible. Don't forget to check your wedge needs when you get new boots. If wedges are unavailable to you, try to purchase boots that are canted correctly for your particular bone structure.

part VI
Especially for Racers

If you want to become an outstanding racer you must begin by developing a sound basic technique. The fine points of racing discussed in this part are only frosting on the cake. Your most important challenge is to master the fundamentals of balance, economy of motion, and ski design utilization discussed in the preceding chapters.

chapter 21
The Sources
of Speed

SKI RACES ARE WON BY COMBINING THE SHORTEST POSSIBLE LINE WITH
THE HIGHEST POSSIBLE SPEED.

To achieve the shortest possible line is easy in theory if not in practice. To develop and maintain the highest possible speed is the ultimate
goal of all racing technique. Three sources of speed are available to
a racer:

1. The pull of gravity.
2. Muscle power.
3. The propelling action of a "bowed" ski.

Attention must be given to each of these elements.

THE PULL OF GRAVITY

Gravity provides the simplest source of speed. Whether you are
schussing a 45-degree slope or standing in a lift line, the pull of gravity
remains constant. *What changes as you ski is the resistance to gravity's
pull.* A steep hill offers less resistance (and hence greater speed) than
a flat hill. On the same slope, a steep traverse angle offers less resistance than a shallow traverse angle. As resistance to gravity decreases, acceleration increases.

Your choice of line determines how efficiently you minimize resistance to the pull of gravity. If all other factors are equal, one racer
can go faster than another by choosing a more efficient line. Choice
of line must be made to provide optimum use of steep terrain, and to
achieve traverse angles as close to the fall line as possible.

It is important to approach flat sections of a race course with maximum possible speed. If there's a short, steep pitch prior to a flat, it's

[145]

(Drawing #28)

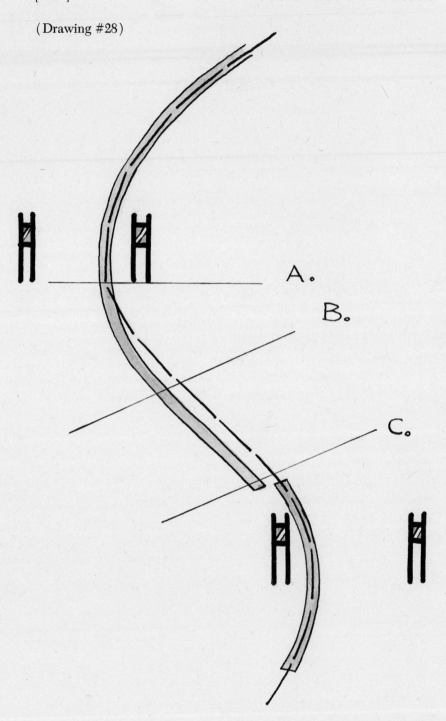

A.

B.

C.

often advantageous to take a longer than direct line, but one that offers maximum use of the steep terrain to provide speed for crossing the flat.

Where there is a shallow traverse between gates, it is best to ski a low line (affording maximum descent angle) until approaching the end of the traverse. Then an uphill skating step will position you for the approaching gate. (See Drawing 28.)

In this diagram, the solid racing line is faster than the dotted line. Between lines A and B the solid line has a steeper angle of descent. Less resistance is offered, so the skier goes faster. The increased speed is maintained from line B to line C, and through the next turn. The uphill step at the end of the traverse positions the skier for gate 3.

When traverses are shorter and closer to the fall line, you can make optimum use of gravity's pull by decreasing the arc of your turns—

(Drawing #29)

letting your downhill ski run close to the fall line—then stepping laterally to the line required for the next gate. This is called lateral projection. (See Drawing 29.)

Lateral projection permits you to stay close to the fall line at the end of each turn—thus increasing your use of gravity for acceleration. The first turn in this drawing shows the track a racer leaves when a lateral step is used. The second turn shows the track of a classic skating turn. This step provides improved line and muscle power acceleration.

MUSCLE POWER

At very slow speeds, poling action will provide acceleration. This uses the muscle power of the arms. At moderate speeds, skating turns provide acceleration whenever a strong push can be achieved with the thrusting leg. In some parallel turns, the power of both legs is used simultaneously to increase pressure on (and then rebound from) the tails of your skis.

Most racers underestimate the importance of muscle power as a source of speed. You must be a strong skater to achieve maximum possible speeds under many race conditions. To appreciate the potentials of muscle power, consider the plight of a speed skater. How does he go fast? *Only* by pushing with his legs—and he develops considerable speed! Equivalent acceleration is available to ski racers whenever they can achieve a stable platform from which to push with one leg. Compromises with balance, line, and wind resistance must, of course, be made.

It is interesting to note that one of the strongest elements of Gustavo Thoeni's racing technique is his frequent use of skating turns and lateral steps. He appears very light on his feet, almost dancing as he steps through slalom gates. Like all great athletes, his movements are so graceful that his power is scarcely evident. But the power is there. Each of Thoeni's little steps increases his speed. If they are skating steps there is forward thrust and direct acceleration. If they are lateral steps, there is no direct acceleration from the step, but greater speed has been obtained by staying close to the fall line. Many stepping movements combine forward thrust and lateral projection.

ACCELERATING FORCE PROVIDED BY YOUR SKIS

The secret of achieving maximum speed from your skis is twofold:
1.   The ski must be bent to a high degree of tension.

2. The tension must be released quickly when pressure is relatively on the tail. This accelerating action of a ski is most easily felt in straight running over bumps. If you press down on the tail of your ski just after your foot crosses the high point of a bump, you bend the tail. When the tail springs straight, it provides acceleration. Maximum acceleration is achieved by applying pressure increasingly toward the tail as the ski flows over the bump. (This is done by pushing your feet ahead as well as down.) Any beginner can do this exercise and feel thrust provided by his ski. For racers, this skill of pushing down on the backside of bumps is particularly exercised in downhill. Accomplished slalom and giant slalom skiers also utilize this technique to gain speed whenever terrain offers the opportunity.

Exactly the same action of a ski that provides acceleration from a bump will provide acceleration from a short-radius turn on smooth terrain.

Instead of pressing on the back of an existing mogul, a racer who makes an accelerating turn creates his own mogul. By applying sufficient edge angle and pressure in a turn, he bends his ski into reverse camber. When the ski straightens out—while on edge and without the tail sliding—it provides acceleration similar to that from a mogul.

To bend a ski to maximum deflection for an accelerating turn, severe edge angle and pressure are required. The tip and tail must be sharp enough to prevent skidding. Pressure distribution on the ski must contribute to the specific work done by the tip and tail at each phase of the turn. To achieve maximum reverse camber, the turn must begin with leverage on the tip. This helps the tip to begin carving, to establish the arc of the turn, and to initiate the reverse camber pattern of the ski. As the tip bends, leverage is moved toward the center of the ski. This is done by the skier's subtly pushing his feet forward (a quicker movement than rocking his body back). This push of the feet also helps the ski to slide forward in its carving track rather than to skid sideways. In the middle phase of the turn, maximum pressure is applied under the boot. Both tip and tail hold equally, and reverse camber is distributed evenly along the length of the ski. As the turn is completed, leverage (and hence pressure) moves toward the tail of the ski. Again, this is controlled by the skier's sliding his feet forward. Pressure is increased throughout the turn by the tightening radius of the turn itself; and, if desired, by extension of the skier's body. At the end of the turn, the back of the ski is "cocked" like a spring by severe pressure and rear leverage.

Release of this spring is the final element in an acceleration turn. At the point where maximum energy is stored in the tail of the ski, it is necessary to *decrease* pressure on the ski. The ski is not strong enough to straighten out while the full pressure of the turn is on it.

Acceleration turns end with a subtle unweighting (contraction, or termination of extension). This lightens the load on the ski and allows it to unbend quickly. The resultant acceleration shoots your skis, feet, and lower legs ahead—*but it does not equally accelerate your whole body.* After the acceleration movement, your body must be "drawn forward" with thigh and stomach muscles to a balanced position over your skis.

In considering the advantages of acceleration turns, you must remember that your whole body does not finally accelerate in the amount your skis do. Your skis and legs (less than one third of your mass) are accelerated; but as soon as they reach extension they are drawn back more than your body is drawn forward. Because your upper-body mass is greater, it dominates the relative adjustment of lower and upper bodies. Some acceleration is gained, but it is finally less than you feel in the moment your skis shoot ahead.

The energy that creates what real acceleration you do gain comes from the spring in the tail of your ski. The energy to cock that spring comes from muscle power as you press on the ski during the turn, and from an effective increase in your body's weight caused by centrifugal force. This also presses on your ski and helps to cock the spring.

In slow-motion films of outstanding acceleration turns, we have studied pressure distribution along a racer's ski. This distribution is clearly visible by noting the point along the ski edge where maximum "edge bite" and snow displacement occur. THE MAXIMUM PRESSURE AT ALL POINTS ALONG THE SKI OCCURS OVER THE SAME SPOT ON THE SNOW. If we dye a six-inch square of snow red and ask an international-class racer to initiate a quick, acceleration turn when his ski tip touches the spot, the following things happen: 1) Maximum tip bite occurs on the red spot. 2) When the skier's foot passes over the red spot, maximum edge bite is under his foot. 3) When the tail of his ski crosses the red spot, maximum pressure is on the tail. Just as the ski tail passes the red spot, the racer reduces down pressure. This allows the ski to accelerate as the turn ends. The ski then tracks in a straight traverse to the following turn. The important points are that the entire edge of the ski passes over the same spot (following its own groove), and maximum pressure throughout the turn remains on the same spot of snow.

This flowing of pressure from tip to tail of the ski has never, to my knowledge, been described in photographs or in print. *It is the key element in perfectly executed short-radius turns.* It explains why, to achieve maximum efficiency from the ski, accelerating turns must begin with forward leverage, and why they end with leverage on the tail. Exception: Turns made close to the fall line with minimal direction change do not require the forward motion. The turn is so limited it can be carved on the tail of the ski. Leverage in such a turn can begin neutral, move aft, and return to neutral. Many racers still prefer to initiate fall-line turns with forward leverage, moving back only to neutral. The turning time is equivalent; recovery time is shortened; balance is upset less; and more precise control of the ski is maintained. The decision to use forward-neutral or neutral-back leverage depends largely on the recovery time available before the next turn. If there is time for recovery, neutral-back is faster because the aft-weighted ski offers less resistance to the snow. If recovery time is limited, it is wise to use forward-neutral leverage and to be perfectly balanced to initiate

Photo
23 A

MALCOLM REISS

23A. *Pete Murphy lets his downhill ski run close to the fall line while stepping up to position himself for the following turn. He effectively minimizes decelerating forces.*

the following turn with precision and control. (Review Photos 13 through 15 and their accompanying text.)

Remember that leverage is changed throughout acceleration turns *not* by moving your hips or center of gravity back, but *by moving your feet ahead.*

Almost all the movements I have described above have been outlined by others under fancy names like "avalement," "jet turns," "S turns," etc. Most people associate these names with body positions. It is better to think about the action of your feet. Avalement is thus not

MALCOLM REISS

23B. By contrast, Ben Hart, who has less ability to carve turns, has turned his skis across the fall line. Serious deceleration results. Ben's skidding downhill ski fails to provide an adequate platform from which to step into the next turn.

so much a sitting-back motion as it is a pushing ahead of your feet, followed by a balance adjustment.

Despite the intriguing nature and potential of acceleration turns, I must end this chapter with a warning. Turns that utilize extreme aft leverage cause major disruptions of balance, and they disturb constant ski contact with the snow. These losses frequently cause more problems than the acceleration gain is worth.

Most racers should give more attention to skiing a smooth line, and using lateral projection to take advantage of gravity acceleration. In ski racing, the fastest total result is often achieved by concentrating on an optimum line, and by minimizing decelerating forces. (See Photos 23A and B.)

Pete Murphy's line at this gate was clearly superior. By completing much of his turn before passing the gate, he did not have to fight Photo centrifugal force and gravity after crossing the fall line. Thus, Murphy 24B makes extremely good use of gravity acceleration, and he achieves a superior sliding action from his skis.

chapter 22

"To Avoid Braking"

The speed of all moving bodies (including ski racers) is determined by the relationship between accelerating and decelerating forces. When accelerating forces are stronger than decelerating forces, speed increases. When decelerating forces are stronger, speed decreases.

THE MOST IMPORTANT ELEMENT IN DETERMINING A SKI RACER'S SPEED IS HIS ABILITY TO MINIMIZE DECELERATING OR BRAKING FORCES. This is more important then developing accelerating forces because, of the three sources of speed identified in the previous chapter, gravity is by far the dominant factor (except on flat terrain). On terrain with adequate pitch for racing, gravity provides at least 80 per cent of the forces accelerating a skier. Because gravity's pull is constant for all racers at the same point on a given course, only 20 per cent of all accelerating forces can be influenced by racer technique. (See Drawing 30.)

By contrast, nearly all influence over decelerating forces is under the direct control of a skier. (See Drawing 31.)

Deceleration potentials range from the minimum drag of a tracking, well-waxed ski to the maximum drag of a sideways skid with a ski 45

(Drawing #30)

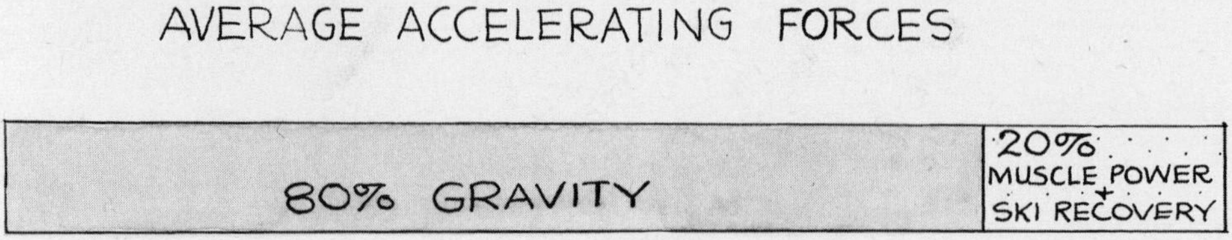

AVERAGE ACCELERATING FORCES

80% GRAVITY	20% MUSCLE POWER + SKI RECOVERY

(Drawing #31)

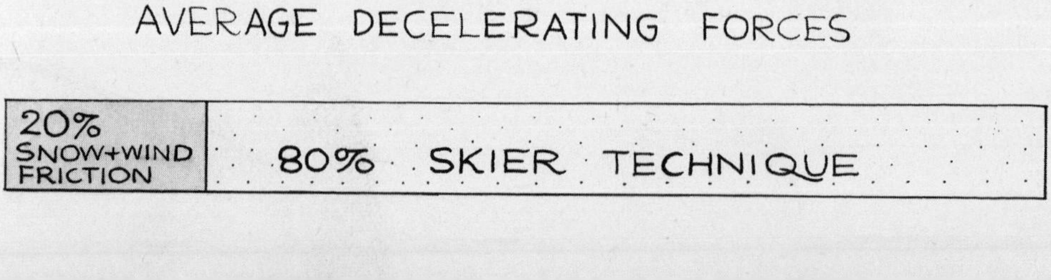

AVERAGE DECELERATING FORCES

20% SNOW+WIND FRICTION	80% SKIER TECHNIQUE

degrees on edge. A PRIMARY GOAL OF RACING TECHNIQUE IS TO MINIMIZE DECELERATING FORCES.

How is this goal achieved? We can begin by restating my one-sentence condensation of this book: "Carve turns, don't slide them." THE MOST IMPORTANT FACTOR IN REDUCING BRAKING EFFECTS IS, VERY SIMPLY, TO MINIMIZE SIDESLIP IN ALL TURNS. Every chapter of this book is related to that goal. Go back to the fundamentals!

Equally important to carving turns is "carving traverses." So much of ski technique is concerned with methods of turning that it's easy to forget the importance of the traverse which links turns together. Traversing, with minimum drag, is essential to a fast racing technique. Traverses comprise more than half of most race courses.

EDGE LOCK

"Edge lock" is one of the most frequently used terms in my coaching vocabulary. It describes a traversing ski with absolutely no sideslip. The ski edge is "locked on" to a tracking course, as securely as a railroad train to its rails. The ski leaves a track in the snow that looks as though a knife-edge were drawn across it. (See Photo 2E.)

Racers must concentrate on edge lock at the critical stage where turns end and traverses begin. During every turn EDGE LOCK MUST BE ACHIEVED AT THE INSTANT YOUR SKIS ARE POINTING IN THE DIRECTION YOU WANT TO GO. There must be no overturning, no momentary skidding at the beginning of each traverse.

There is a close relationship between edge lock and all accelerating turns. At the instant the ski is neutralized at the end of a turn, precise edge lock must be achieved. In a well-carved turn, edge lock exists throughout the turn in the carving track of the ski. The transition from carving turn to "carving traverse" is easy. In sharp turns that involve steering to achieve direction change, it is more difficult to make the transition from a skidding ski (in the turn) to edge lock in the traverse. A quick edge-set combined with a forward push of your feet is often required.

The earlier edge lock is achieved in each traverse, the greater percentage of the traverse distance is covered at maximum speed. Therefore, the racer who consistently achieves edge lock at the earliest point after each turn will carry the greatest speed.

Diagrammed in Drawing 32 are the tracks left in the snow by three racers of descending ability. The arrows indicate where *edge lock* is achieved in each traverse.

If you remember my opening remarks in this book about watching a racers skis to measure his ability, you can best appreciate the sig-

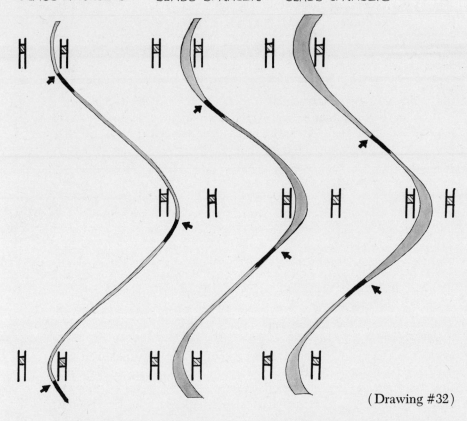

(Drawing #32)

nificance of these diagrams. The tracks your skis leave in the snow represent the end result of your technique. All other motions are input to technique. *What your skis finally do in the snow is what counts!* When they skid, you slow down. When they track, you go faster. Given equal accelerating forces, the skier whose technique provides minimum resistance goes the fastest.

I can stand blindfolded beside a slalom or a giant slalom course and tell how fast each racer is going. I listen! Wide areas in the above diagrams produce skidding sounds. A carving track produces almost no sound at all. When free-skiing with a group of racers whom I know well, I can identify each by the "sound" of his technique. Pressure, timing, balance on his skis—each produces its own sound, and every racer's skis create distinctive "tunes" on the snow.

CHATTERING

The nemesis of all ski racers is "chattering"—skidding in turns and traverses when they want to be on a carving or a tracking ski. On easy courses, where the beginner chatters frequently, an Olympic competitor can ski with no chatter or skidding at all. But at ascending levels of competition, courses are set on more challenging terrain. When icy conditions prevail, the world's best skiers often slide and chatter well below the line they plan to hold.

It's not surprising, therefore, that the most frequently asked question at coaching clinics is: "How can I stop chattering?" I'm aware of only one satisfactory answer, given in Hanover by former Olympian Brooks Dodge—"Don't begin!"

There is much wisdom in this blunt remark. We are bound, always, by the laws of physics: In this case by the law that states "a body in motion will tend in the same direction at the same velocity until acted upon by additional forces." Because of ski design, the necessary forces to change direction are easily employed so long as a ski continues in a carving action. A skidding ski, however, offers less potential for direction change. Once your skis break into a skid on a southerly course, it's difficult to redirect them to an easterly heading.

The situation described here is similar to that encountered in an automobile. As long as the tires maintain tracking adhesion to the pavement, controlled turns are easily made. But once the tires "break loose" and a skid begins, it is difficult to regain precise directional control. The breaking loose of the car is identical to a skier breaking from the track of a carved turn into a chattering skid. It's easier to avoid skidding than to stop skidding. Back to fundamentals! And to round turns!

You must understand that the smallest amount of skid at any point in a turn or traverse greatly increases your chances of skidding at the following point. That's why it is so important to carve turns well— and *particularly to begin turns with a carving action.* Edge your ski first, then turn it! Particularly in giant slalom, many racers try to turn too sharp. They go too straight at the poles, thus requiring a skidded turn. It's faster to stay on a rounder line, but not skid. Especially, it is important not to force the turn under the pole. Let your skis run and use a lateral step to reach the next gate. Review Photos 23A and 23B.

Racers who begin turns with even minimal skidding action at the tail of their skis initiate a chain of events far more drastic than the first error. One of the fascinations of snow-ski racing is that each mistake you make creates a potential for more serious mistakes.

Terrain factors can increase the penalty for skidding off line. Gates are often set so that only a perfect turn keeps a racer clear of fall-away or bumpy terrain. This is one reason that total control throughout a race course often leads to victory. Five accelerating turns followed by a single turn with loss of balance and line will produce a slower total than six smooth, precise turns.

Billy Kidd, 1970 FIS Combined Champion, was not an especially gifted athlete. He won ski races not on raw athletic ability (strength, balance, and coordination) but on precision—on mastery of line and reduction of mistakes. The secret to Kidd's success was always in minimizing decelerating forces rather than accentuating accelerating forces.

The final speed of a racer is a resultant of the balance between accelerating and decelerating forces. Racers and coaches must give more attention to reducing braking effects at all points in turns and traverses.

WAX AND WIND

Two factors offer continual decelerating force to the racer. First is the natural friction between his skis and the snow. This friction can never be eliminated; it can be reduced by expert waxing, and by proper maintenance of the ski base and edges. Every effort to reduce this friction must be made not only for racing, but for training sessions as well.

In the past decade, great strides have been made to reduce wind resistance. Tighter clothes of low-drag materials have been developed. Wind-tunnel tests have been made to determine optimum downhill positions. The basic findings of these tests have been published elsewhere, and need not be repeated here. Any racer who wants to appreciate the importance of reducing wind drag need only stick his arm out an automobile window when traveling 40 to 60 miles per hour. Simply turning the hand palm forward or palm down creates a substantial difference in drag. Most racers appreciate this fact and strive to minimize wind drag in downhill and giant slalom racing.

Much publicity has been given to the "egg position" and other aspects of reducing wind resistance, while equally important factors of ski resistance in downhill and giant slalom have been neglected. It is difficult to carve good turns while maintaining a low downhill crouch. Forward leverage, agility, and balance are all restricted. The more erect a skier's stance, the more precisely he can carve turns and reduce ski drag. For all racing situations, compromises must be made to provide the lowest total drag when wind and ski resistance are combined. For many racers, a higher stance than they normally assume will provide the lowest total drag.

Despite the hoopla given to the French "egg position" throughout the 1960's, Karl Schranz was the best downhill skier of the decade. I have studied numerous films of international downhills which Schranz won while standing more erect than his principal competitors. His record was particularly impressive on the most difficult courses. Downhills are seldom won on the straightaways. Winners are decided in the turns; and it was in the turns that Schranz excelled. He consistently sacrificed minimum wind drag to gain a position on his skis that allowed him to more efficiently carve turns, and to reduce deceleration caused by skidding.

What Schranz sensed better than his competition was that ski friction can be greater than wind friction. He never hesitated to stand as erect as was necessary to carve his turns perfectly. Unfortunately, neither coaches nor computers can tell racers how erect they should stand for any given turn. Each competitor must develop a sixth sense to properly judge the comparative effects of wind and ski drag. In emphasizing the relative importance of ski drag I do not mean to imply that wind drag is unimportant. Wind drag is critical—but the action of the ski in the snow is *more* critical. In writing about his FIS downhill victory at Portillo, Killy said: "It's how you make your turns that really determines your speed down the mountain."

It is my opinion that a majority of world-class racers (including most of the U.S. Team) are currently skiing giant slalom in too low a crouch. In doing so, they decrease their agility and balance, and they decrease the efficiency with which they carve turns. A fairly low position should be used on fast, easy sections of giant slalom courses, but when the going gets tough—when difficult turns must be made over challenging terrain—an erect stance is preferable. (Review the pictures of giant slalom turns throughout this book.)

In slalom, speeds are sufficiently slow and turning requirements so continuous that wind effects are of minimal concern. Still, they are important. Racing parkas, not sweaters, should be worn for slalom events. The difference in drag may cause a gain of only a few hundredths of a second. That's a significant gain in many races today.

A complete awareness of wind resistance must account for the differences in racing against a headwind, or with a tailwind. If there's a tailwind of 20 MPH for slalom, wind drag is no factor at all. If the tailwind exceeds the course speed a fat down parka should be worn during competition. When tailwinds exist for giant slalom and downhill, racers may adjust to a higher stance permitting optimum ski control. If strong headwinds prevail, a lower-than-normal stance must be used, and awareness of wind drag must dominate the choice of stance. I have frequently seen downhills run in headwinds of 30 MPH. Added to a 60-MPH course speed, this produces a 90-MPH "air speed" for the competitor. Aerodynamic body positions then assume enormous significance.

chapter 23
Running Gates

The greatest fascination of racing is that there are so many variables —in terrain, speed, line, snow conditions, etc. It's impossible to cover every kind of turn that will confront a racer in a single season, or even in one race. The best I can do here is to stress the fundamentals common to most turns. Each racer must develop judgment through experience, and must learn what compromises produce the best total result. Here are the important fundamentals:

PRACTICE

Run thousands and thousands of gates. Develop a training area with fast lift service that lets you run as many gates per hour per training session as possible. Don't climb courses to "get in shape." There are better ways to get in shape. Use time on the hill to "pass poles."

Bad training is worse than no training. When you get tired or sloppy, quit. Don't practice bad habits. Stop training when you are making good runs. When you're tired, you reinforce bad habits in muscle-coordination-memory patterns. If you're having a bad day, leave the course, take a few "hot dogging" runs on the mountain, do some slow maneuvers, then come back to the gates. If you're still uncoordinated, go free-skiing, work on your equipment, or go home to bed.

Try to do half your training on full-length courses. The concentration and rhythm required by sixty gates is very different from that required by twenty gates. When running long courses, be sure to finish most runs. You must stand up to win ski races! It makes no sense to practice at speeds you can't sustain. Learn your limits, and ski within them.

To learn new skills, it's necessary to try things you haven't mastered —to exceed your limits of full control. One quarter to one third of your training should be spent in this manner; but know when you are doing it! If your goal is to go as fast as you can till you fall, that's fine—

just be sure both you and your coach are consciously working on that approach. When you shift gears to making standing runs, shift completely. Otherwise you train recklessly and learn little more than how to be confused about your own intentions, and how to fall down.

Spend some time running short courses (ten to twenty gates) that allow you to concentrate on making a few excellent turns. If there is one particularly difficult turn, run it over and over again with total concentration until you master it.

Before you can make sixty good turns you must learn to make one. The Cochran family have many things going for them, but the most important factor in their racing success is that they know how to make one good turn. On the short hill behind their home in Richmond, Vermont, they have spent countless hours learning to use the full design potential of their skis. That is the foundation on which all great racers are built. It's often learned more thoroughly on a ten-gate hill than on a bigger slope. One gets tired of ten gates unless he's a perfectionist; then ten gates continue to provide a challenge. The Cochrans are perfectionists, and that's why they win. They have, of course, moved far beyond their small hill to the variety of challenges that big mountains offer. They have met those challenges with two priceless attributes: an instinct for perfection, and a full understanding of their relationship to their skis.

LINE

It is impossible to dictate a proper line to every racer. Each competitor is limited by his equipment and by his technique. The best line for Racer A may be an impossibility for Racer B. What are the basic factors each racer must consider in choosing his line?

1. The shortest distance between two points is a straight line. Take the straightest line possible between gates *without sacrificing speed by turning so sharply that deceleration results. The key element in choosing line is that you must maintain speed.* If you approach a gate at 30 MPH, you want to turn without slowing to 28. Ideally you want to accelerate to 32. This means you must *carve turns.* If an accelerating turn is possible, use it—but don't sacrifice too much balance and control. Whenever possible use a stepping motion (lateral projection) to decrease the angle of each turn, and to provide greater acceleration from gravity.

2. For gates set close to the fall line, the straighter line you take, the fewer degrees you must turn. The straighter line is easier. Class A racers can run fall-line gates with much less effort than Class C

racers simply because the A line requires so much less turning. The timid or unskilled racer, by skiing a wider line, increases the width and difficulty of his course. It takes courage to charge gates straight on, because greater speeds result; but turning requirements are simplified. When close to the fall line, have courage and charge.

3. When gates are set across the fall line, requiring turns of 30 to 90 degrees, the straightest line between gates requires the shortest radius turn at each pole. Often a longer line is faster as the radius of each turn is increased.

For this kind of turn, the skill of each racer becomes a key factor in choosing his line. Each competitor must judge what turns he can make in a quick carving motion, and what turns will require a longer arc. Especially in giant slalom, it is important to make round turns that minimize braking effects. Long turns—following a smooth arc— are preferable for maintaining speed. To make a proper choice of line, you must often consider the different effects of gravity at the beginning, the middle, and the end of turns. (See Drawing 33.)

In Phase I of the turn in Drawing 33 gravity exerts a force toward the inside of the turn. This partially neutralizes centrifugal force.

(Drawing #33)

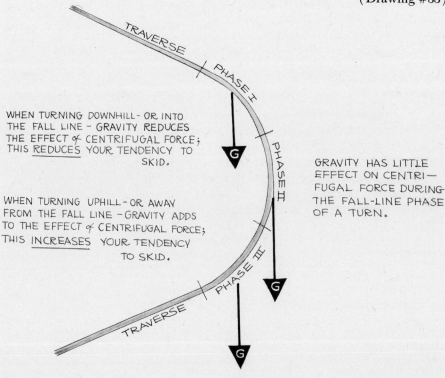

WHEN TURNING DOWNHILL- OR INTO THE FALL LINE – GRAVITY REDUCES THE EFFECT of CENTRIFUGAL FORCE; THIS REDUCES YOUR TENDENCY TO SKID.

WHEN TURNING UPHILL- OR AWAY FROM THE FALL LINE –GRAVITY ADDS TO THE EFFECT of CENTRIFUGAL FORCE; THIS INCREASES YOUR TENDENCY TO SKID.

GRAVITY HAS LITTLE EFFECT ON CENTRI— FUGAL FORCE DURING THE FALL-LINE PHASE OF A TURN.

In Phase II, or the fall-line phase of the turn, gravity has little effect on increasing or reducing the tendency to skid. However, as you pass through the fall line, gravity does provide acceleration which will increase centrifugal force in the third phase of the turn.

In Phase III of the turn, both gravity and centrifugal force tend to pull you outside the desired arc of your turn.

Consider the implications of Drawing 33.

(A) It is easier to turn without skidding in the first phase of the turn than in the third phase.

(B) In turns requiring a major change of direction, it is advisable to make your turns on a high line, rather than to charge straight at a gate and turn sharply underneath it.

(C) The sharpest part of your turns should be made in Phase I and Phase II, where gravity does not compound the tendency to skid.

(D) The speed gained in Phase II must be carried through Phase III and into the traverse.

(E) Lengthening the radius of turns as you progress into Phase III helps to accomplish (D).

(F) Any rounding of a turn (lengthening the radius) in Phases I and II also lengthens the radius of turn required in Phase III. This reduces skidding tendencies in Phase III and in the following traverse.

(G) Any way you can lengthen Phase II is helpful because it increases the time period when gravity acceleration has the greatest effect. Thus it increases your speed.

How can you prolong Phase II? By staying in the fall line longer—and using a lateral projection to reach the traverse line required to approach the next gate.

4. In the final analysis, all factors of line are determined by how well a skier can maintain his momentum. Review Chapters 21 and 22, and use your judgment to balance the many factors that contribute to speed. Remember the control of decelerating forces is more important than accelerating forces. You must make sharp turns to maintain the shortest possible line, but you must avoid excessive braking effects. The wise racer often lets his skis run on a fairly long arc to maintain speed. This is especially useful where a sharp turn is followed by an easy turn. It is wise not to force the difficult turn; maintain momentum and don't worry if you approach the easier gate on a low line. As the turn there is easy, you can catch up. The opposite situation—an easy turn followed by a sharp one—often requires that you set up a little in the easy gate to reduce the difficulty of the harder turn that follows.

5. When running gates on soft snow, extreme care must be taken not to force turns. A consistent pressure must be kept on the skis at all times. Turns must be smooth and round. Acceleration turns or very

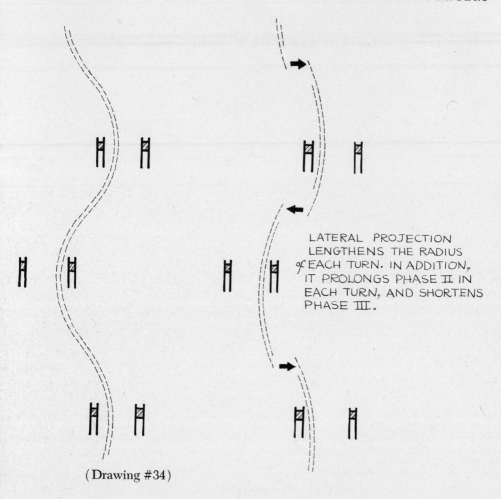

LATERAL PROJECTION
LENGTHENS THE RADIUS
of EACH TURN. IN ADDITION,
IT PROLONGS PHASE II IN
EACH TURN, AND SHORTENS
PHASE III.

(Drawing #34)

sharp turns both require extreme pressure to bend the ski into reverse camber. The application of this pressure pushes the ski deep into the snow, causing unacceptable braking effects. Long, round turns produce the fastest result in soft snow conditions. The skier must be light and delicate on his skis. Even step turns must be made gingerly to avoid pushing the thrusting ski too deep into the snow. Similarly, under very icy conditions where it is difficult to avoid skidding, the long arcing turn is often preferable to a tighter turn that risks skidding. Maintain momentum!

6.   When a course is rutted, you have two alternatives; stay inside the rut, or go all the way to the outside. It's preferable to stay inside the rut if you have sufficient skill to do so, if there is a wide enough ledge to turn on, and if the ledge is not so steep as to make a fall-away turn.

If these three conditions do not exist, it is usually wise to "ride the rut"—to use the outside bank like a bobsled run. Although the line at the outside of the bank may be far from the pole, the smooth banked turns provide minimum deceleration opportunities. The important thing is to decide early that you intend to ride the outside of a rut, and then enter the turn on the outside of the bank where the rut begins. Unskilled racers charge straight into a rut so their ski tips go into the deepest part of the hole, and then abruptly hit the outside wall. This causes instant deceleration and loss of balance. This error probably

Photo 24

PHOTOPRESS

24. *In this turn, which requires extreme angulation, Augert's skis pass more than 3 feet from the pole.*

causes 70 per cent of all falls on rutted courses. Like an auto racer "coming down off the wall" at the end of a banked turn, a good skier may often cut out of a rut by coming off the wall before the low end of the rut is reached. This can only be done if there is no severe hole at the end of the rut, and if the turn was begun at the right place.

Running ruts is a very special art that should be frequently practiced. Learn to make the rut work for you. Don't fight against it. Always respect the danger of injury that deep ruts present. When the troughs get too deep, reset the course.

BODY AND POLE

Under most course conditions, racers should attempt to pass as close as possible to every pole. By doing so, they reduce the effective width of their racing line. Total distance between gates is shortened, and the degrees of arc required for each turn are reduced.

When thinking of getting "close to the poles," remember that the path of your skis is not the same as the path of your body. *Your skis must always pass far enough from each pole to allow sufficient inward lean to provide balance in the turn and angulation to edge your skis.* For turns requiring 45 to 60 degrees of inward lean you must choose a ski track as much as two or three feet away from the pole. (See Photos 24 and 25.)

Photo 25

If your outside foot must pass thirty inches from a pole to allow for inward lean and angulation, then the tip of your outside ski must pass the same thirty inches from the pole; and your approach to the gate must be on a carving arc aimed thirty inches from the pole. Remember that in a carved turn, the whole ski edge must pass through the same groove.

A common error of many racers is that of aiming their skis too close to slalom and giant slalom poles. If your tips are aimed ten inches from a pole, and your feet must pass thirty inches from the pole, then you must slide twenty inches sideways to get your feet away from the pole. This means you will skid at the critical area of each turn just prior to passing the pole; and you are likely still to be skidding *after* you pass the pole.

You must always plan the line of your skis to allow for the inward lean each turn requires. Slalom turns close to the fall line require little inward lean, and so may permit a path of the ski eight or ten inches from the pole. High-speed giant slalom turns often require eighteen to thirty-six inches of space for inward lean. Every turn is different. Racers must adjust.

25. *In a more moderate turn, Biechu carves his line more than 30 inches from the pole.*

One of the principal causes of aiming too straight at poles is that your skis follow your eyes; and most racers focus their eyes on the base of upcoming poles. They should focus on the exact line their skis should follow, studying the snow conditions they will encounter. Racers who do this correctly seldom catch a tip on a pole. When approaching the gate diagrammed in Drawing 35, a racer's eyes should focus on the track his skis will follow—the dark line in the diagram. Even at world-class levels—in the first seed of giant slalom—there is a marked difference in the line on which slalom specialists approach giant slalom gates and the line the best giant slalom skiers use. The giant slalom winners consistently choose a rounder line farther from the pole—making a more purely carved turn. The slalom specialists— by habit of passing closer to slalom poles—often aim too close and skid into many giant slalom turns.

If a racer does not allow sufficient room for inward lean at a pole— and he does not skid his feet away from the pole—then he must duck his body and decrease his angulation at the moment he passes it.

Any ducking of the body is a contraction or down-unweighting movement. It takes pressure off the skis, reducing reverse camber, and seriously affecting ski performance in a carved turn.

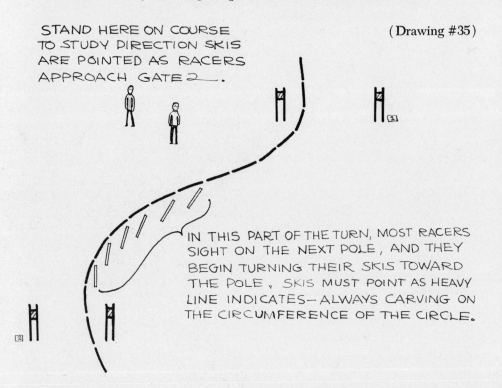

STAND HERE ON COURSE
TO STUDY DIRECTION SKIS
ARE POINTED AS RACERS
APPROACH GATE 2 .

(Drawing #35)

IN THIS PART OF THE TURN, MOST RACERS
SIGHT ON THE NEXT POLE, AND THEY
BEGIN TURNING THEIR SKIS TOWARD
THE POLE, SKIS MUST POINT AS HEAVY
LINE INDICATES—ALWAYS CARVING ON
THE CIRCUMFERENCE OF THE CIRCLE.

PHOTOPRESS

26A and B. *These sequence photos of the French racer Serrat show the problems caused by aiming the tips too close to a gate. Note the difference in angulation as Serrat approaches the pole, and just after passage. He had to flatten his skis to slide away from the pole. His inside ski has been so squeezed that his tips have nearly crossed. To duck by the pole he has had to bend so low at the waist that he sacrifices quickness and strength in his skiing stance.*

Photos
26A, 26B

A

B

27A and B. *Two unidentified racers at the Junior Nationals pass too close to the giant slalom pole. Study the effect that ducking the pole has on their skis. Edge angle and pressure are seriously disturbed. A weak position offering poor agility results; this hampers the completion of this turn and the initiation of the following turn.*

C

D

MALCOLM REISS

27C and D. By contrast, the young Canadian, Sean Russell, and Pam Noyes from Burke Mountain pass the same gate very cleanly. Angulation, pressure, leverage, balance, line, strength of stance, and momentum are easily maintained. Pam Noyes, fifteen, is Eastern Women's Giant Slalom Champion. She finished fourth in this Junior National race.

Photos 27A, B, C, D

A racer who decreases his angulation decreases the edge angle of his skis. This reduces the carving potential of his skis and induces a skid —just at the critical moment when he is passing the pole.

In fact, most racers who try to pass too close to poles suffer both of the above difficulties. They lose both pressure and edge angle, and thus they skid past the pole. All but the very best racers in the world repeatedly make this mistake unless they have been carefully trained not to. To appreciate the truth of these remarks, you have only to watch the skis of racers approaching and passing the poles in any giant slalom race.

The best giant slalom skiers in the world seldom strike a pole; they take a line so "clean" of the gates they are not required to duck or to take their skis off edge as they pass each gate. Thus they maintain their momentum in more purely carved turns.

The same basic rules apply to slalom. Your skis must be aimed the exact distance from each pole that your feet must pass to provide required angulation. Because slalom speeds are slower, and turns are often closer to the fall line, the average turn requires less angulation and inward lean. Any ducking at the pole is equally wrong in slalom, as it decreases pressure on the skis at a critical point in the turn.

To maintain consistent edge angle and pressure on your skis, you must run gates in such a way that the gates do not dictate the motions of your body.

Hitting poles creates deceleration, and disturbs a racer's balance. The few inches of line that are gained by striking poles are seldom worth the price that is paid.

Although many racers feel agressive and "fast" when striking poles, the simple laws of physics guarantee that speed is lost. It takes energy to move the pole; and that energy comes from the forward momentum of the racer. Especially on flat sections, one stiff pole on the shoulder can reduce a racer's speed by 3 or 4 MPH. The resulting deceleration is clearly visible to even a casual spectator.

The simple fact is that the world's best slalom skiers try not to hit poles. Because they ski a very tight line, they do brush poles fairly often. But they *brush* them. They don't hit them head on. Most of the time they don't intend even to brush. I have seen films of World Cup slalom and giant slalom races where the winner never touched a pole. The most important task in racing is to follow a perfect line with your skis, to be under total control and in perfect balance at all times. My advice is to ski a clean line and to concentrate on making your skis go fast over the snow.

MALCOLM REISS

28A and B. Bruce Maxwell, a Northern Rocky Mountain skier, cuts so close to a slalom gate that serious loss of speed and balance must occur from striking the pole.

 Peter Dodge, on his way to winning the first run of the Junior National Slalom, is close to the pole, but does not strike it. Dodge, a Burke Mountain racer, has been trained to run slalom courses as cleanly as possible. In this photo, Peter exhibits a strong position on his skis: his knees are bent enough to provide a wide range of movement for edge control and angulation. His back is relatively straight. His hips are almost square—turned just slightly as he turns his upper body a moderate amount to get close to the pole and narrow his line to the next gate.

Photos
28A, 28B

28C. Striking poles causes deceleration and loss of precise ski control.

There are occasional times when pole contact is acceptable.

1.   It is acceptable to brush the *downhill side* of a pole with your fore-arm. This is striking the backside of the pole. Deceleration does not result, and balance loss is minimal as your body is moving away from the pole when your arm strikes it. Some racers display excessive in and out arm movements—apparently to brush poles aside with a lateral sweep of their forearms. Quieter use of the arms is preferable in developing a sound technique. Breaststroke motions are best left in swimming pools.

2.   There are occasional course situations when a pole should be in-tentionally and vigorously displaced. If there is a marked advantage to skiing a very tight line, and if the poles are set in loose snow, the pole can be "removed."

There are three secrets to keeping your body clear of a pole while keeping your skis on a close line. The first secret is to turn your shoul-ders sideways (inside shoulder ahead). This narrows your upper body. Some racers call this "getting your back against the pole." (See Photos

4 and 25.) It helps to ski a tight line but the upper-body movement detracts from normal turning technique. A compromise between balance requirements must be made. Moderation is wise. You should simply choose a line far enough from the pole to avoid hitting it with your arm or shoulders. (See Photos 29A and B, on next page.)

The second hint to clearing poles is to maintain an erect stance. Many racers bend forward at the waist to get their shoulders more quickly by each pole. To balance this upper body lean, their hips must move back. As their hips are the last part of their bodies to pass the pole, they are in a worse position after leaning forward. An erect stance improves your balance, agility, and timing; and it gets your body most quickly by the pole. (See Photo 30.)

TIMING YOUR TURN AT THE POLE

In this discussion we must distinguish between three distinct kinds of turns:

Photo
29 C

1. Long round turns of a sustained nature.
2. Quick, short (acceleration) turns made close to the fall line.
3. Those turns with a duration and arc between the first two categories.

It is impossible to separate the timing of long rounded turns from the broader subject of line. Each turn is a flowing motion linked smoothly with connecting traverses. There is no dynamic beginning to the turn. A subtle change of edge and gradual application of turning pressure directs the ski on a smooth arc around each gate. The success of this kind of turn depends on two elements: First, the minimizing of decelerating forces; and second, the selection of optimum line. Both subjects have been discussed elsewhere and need not be repeated here.

Quick turns of limited arc require the most precise timing. A short turn is like a standing broadjump: It requires one quick, coordinated movement. You prepare for it by being in perfect balance—then your body energy is collected, compressed, and exploded in a unified motion. When the movement is ended, your energy is spent. The entire motion is determined by the first movement. This is similar to swinging a baseball bat. You cock the bat; and then swing. The swing is one motion, developing maximum force at the time you meet the ball. Once the swing begins, there's no stopping it.

MALCOLM REISS

29A, B. Lyndall Heyer, a 15-year-old Burke Mountain Academy student, is the 1972 Junior National Slalom Champion. Shown here on her first run, she demonstrates the conservative style which has made her a consistent slalom winner. She is almost always in perfect balance, skiing with quiet arm and body movements. She's steady, precise, always on line. She does not allow the pole to seriously affect her skiing stance. Sarah Pendleton shows the same discipline. Note the reverse camber in Sarah's ski. She is carving a smooth turn, maintaining momentum. She will not change her body position to pass the pole. Already she is looking ahead to the next gate. She concentrates on her continuing line more than on the adjacent pole.

Photos 29A, 29B, 30

30. Compare the erect stance of Leith Lende here to the waist-bent position of Serrat in Photo 26B. Leith's inside hip will clear the pole earlier, as it is farther forward. Despite the aggressive arm action shown here, Leith's stance is basically conservative. She won the second run of the 1972 Junior National Slalom.

MALCOLM REISS

(Drawing #36)

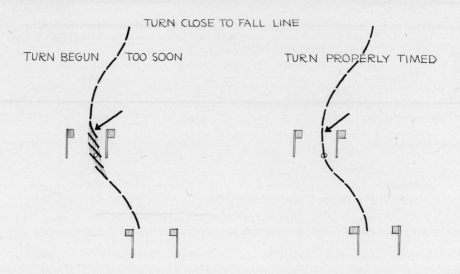

TURN CLOSE TO FALL LINE

TURN BEGUN   TOO SOON

TURN PROPERLY TIMED

AT ARROW, SKIS ARE AIMED AT POLE;
BUT RACER'S FEET MUST PASS OVER
CIRCLE TO LEAVE ROOM FOR ANGULATION.
RACER MUST FLATTEN SKIS AND SKID
TO CIRCLE.

AT ARROW, RACER'S SKIS ARE
AIMED AT CIRCLE. CARVED
TURN RESULTS.

When a skier desires to make a quick, short turn, he must initiate it at precisely the right time. If he turns too early, he is left like a ballplayer swinging at a change-up pitch. His swing is complete, but the ball isn't there yet. For the skier, his turn is complete, but the gate isn't there yet. All he can do is flatten his skis and let them skid sideways until he reaches the pole. Then he can edge and hope he doesn't chatter too long before getting edge lock toward the next gate. His turn is a failure because he expended his energy too soon.

At what point must the turn begin? *When making quick, short turns near the fall line, you must delay each turn until the tips of your skis are even with or past the pole.* This allows your ski tip (and hence your body) to follow a path equidistant from the pole. Remember that to reduce skidding your boots should pass as close as possible over the line traced by the tip of your ski. You must not begin turns so early as to cause your ski tips to cut closer to the pole than your feet should pass. (See Drawing 36.)

By delaying the major body motions until after passing the pole, many complications are removed for the racer. Especially important—the racer who thus delays his turn need never worry about straddling poles or catching the tip of his inside ski. The cause of straddling is beginning turns too early, and either carving or skidding toward the pole *before* passing it.

Perhaps the majority of racing turns fall between the extremes discussed. They are neither long and smooth, nor are they of such limited arc they can be made in one motion. For all these middle-radius turns, the elements of short and long turns must be combined. First, the dynamic movement of a short turn must initiate the direction change of the skis; then the art of "just standing properly on the ski" must be used to complete the turn.

To time such turns the line chosen must be exactly right. The turn will begin before gate passage. The racer must select the best arc for

(Drawing #37)

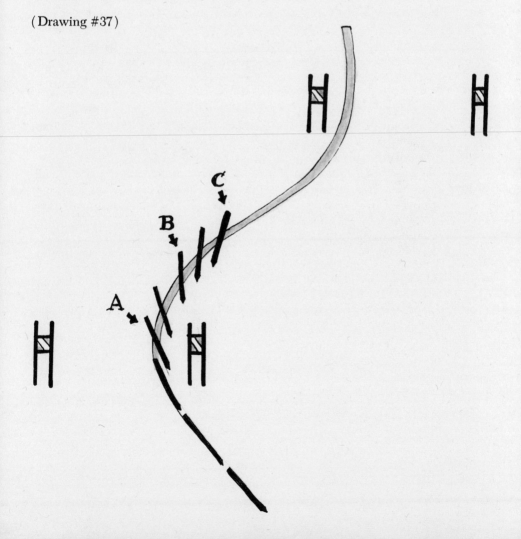

the turn—one that combines maximum carving opportunity with shortest distance. If too tight a line is chosen, an excessive skid results. If too long a line is chosen, the racer simply goes too far.

After choosing the optimum line, the turn must not be started until the latest moment that can produce the desired line. Drawing 37 shows a medium-radius giant slalom turn. The gray line represents the optimum arc for this turn. *Speed is so high that even the best skiers will skid to some degree.* But a Class A skier will begin skidding at line A; a Class B skier at line B; and a Class C skier at line C. Less skilled racers begin turns of this type much too early, skidding before they reach the gate. When they finally reach point A they have no dynamic energy left. They are like the baseball player who swings too early.

When analyzing common mistakes, coaches must consider why racers continually make them. In the case of beginning turns too early it is a combination of needing security, and of trying to maintain a "high line" or "stay ahead of the course." Confronted by a difficult turn, racers with less than total confidence will initiate a turn early to get a head start on meeting its challenge. It's human nature to do so. I define this error as "feeling your way into a turn." That's what a racer is doing—feeling his way, testing snow conditions. By skidding at the start of the turn, the racer actually increases his problems; although the braking effect allows him to complete the turn at a slower (and easier) speed.

The ideal solution for this problem is simply to delay the initiation of each turn as long as possible while staying on a desired line. If a racer lacks sufficient turning ability, he must choose a rounder line. Racers and coaches must give special attention to this error of "feeling their way into turns." It's a fault common to all but world-class competitors. My studies of Can-Am films in 1971 showed almost every girl skidding into difficult slalom and giant slalom turns. A majority of the boys frequently committed the same mistake. If they had the courage to wait longer, and then use all of their energy constructively, these racers could more perfectly carve turns which they now are skidding.

chapter 24
Terrain for Training

It's important to train on every kind of terrain you might encounter in race conditions. Many racing programs are limited to one area for setting gates. If this is so, you must free-ski, and simulate course conditions on terrain different from your practice hill.

It's especially important to practice on very steep hills, and on flat areas too. Steep terrain scares many racers simply because they have no experience with it. To develop the skills required for maintaining a good line on steep terrain, only a short pitch is necessary. When you learn to make one perfect turn, it's easy enough to make ten.

Gordi Eaton, former U.S. men's coach, believes one reason the Swiss team is perennially strong in giant slalom is because they do a lot of high-speed free-skiing on bumpy terrain. Balance, agility, and quick reflexes are certainly developed. Confidence increases for high-speed turns. It's important, when free-skiing, that you work at all times to obtain optimum speed from your skis. Be precise in every movement. Simulate giant slalom racing lines. Try never to let your skis skid. Be loose and relaxed. Ski full-mountain, nonstop runs.

There's an old adage in racing that "you stay alive on the steep, and you win on the flats." The greatest opportunities for step turns and muscle power acceleration are offered on flat terrain. Racers who have developed these special skills reap big rewards. Competitors should sometimes train on long courses averaging as little as 10 per cent grade. On flat terrain, gates are usually spread well apart, offering the racer maximum freedom to execute accelerating maneuvers without loss of line or balance. It takes practice to go fast on the flat. The flatter the terrain becomes, the higher percentage of accelerating forces can be influenced by a racer. In running dual slaloms on a hill steep at the top and flat on the bottom, we see most races lost by a bad mistake on the steep, or won by special skills on the flat.

It is important not only to select varying terrain for training courses, but also to set courses at varying speeds. Racers should practice slow traversing courses, and fast fall-line courses and every combination of both. Regardless of what you or your coach thinks is a good course, you must practice every kind of course you can logically expect to race on.

chapter 25
Specific Turns

I have avoided the impulse throughout this book to write separately of downhill, giant slalom, and slalom. I have done so to simplify the book, and because I believe the fundamentals of ski control and balance are identical for all kinds of turns. Once those fundamentals are mastered, an intelligent racer can apply them to turns of every speed and radius. What follows here are a few hints about common turns that will be helpful to developing racers.

SLALOM

The quick, short-radius slalom turn has been exhaustively analyzed in chapters on acceleration and running gates. I would emphasize here that slalom must still be a fluid event, requiring forty or fifty linked turns. The racer who best maintains momentum and a steady rhythm wins many slalom races.

GIANT SLALOM: THE LONG SMOOTH TURN

In order to carve long turns of sustained radius it is necessary that you find a balanced position on your skis that will create a constant turning force. This kind of turn is antithetical to the dynamic motion of a quick slalom turn. Every effort should be made to stand quietly —to feel the snow—to remain square over your skis. Subtle adjustments of knee and ankle position control edge angle and leverage. Remember to "work your skis over bumps" when terrain permits: Lighten your skis as the tips contact a bump, and press the tails on the back side of bumps.

For medium-radius turns, your weight should be carried mostly on your downhill ski. This increases the effective pressure on the ski, permitting you to bend the ski into reverse camber. Use your uphill ski for balance by keeping it in light contact with the snow. On some

[183]

fast, long, bumpy turns you might carry up to 30 per cent of your weight on the inside ski to maintain better balance.

DOWNHILL TURNS

The primary challenge of downhill turns is to maintain the carving action of your ski at very high speeds and against relatively strong centrifugal forces. Constant pressure must be kept on the tip of the ski to keep contact with the snow, and to keep the tip establishing the arc of the turn.

It is difficult to maintain forward leverage and sufficient edging from a tuck position. A fairly high hip position is required to maintain adequate forward leverage on your ski. The very best downhillers come dynamically forward on their skis for maximum effort turns. Less accomplished skiers remain too far back. A downhill ski has a less severe side-cut and a softer tip than slalom or giant slalom skis. Extra effort must be made to keep the skis carving well in demanding turns.

Many downhillers use a very wide stance for long, fast turns where they are trying to maintain a tuck position. They are thus able to roll the downhill ski well on edge by pressing the downhill knee far to the inside of the turn. Balance is maintained by carrying some weight on the inside ski. (See Photos 2A, B, C, and D.)

STEP TURNS

The most neglected skill in ski racing (and in recreational skiing) is the development of step turns. Man is a two-legged animal. He runs comfortably stepping from one foot to the other. Stepping maneuvers on snow skis should be equally natural.

Step turns have two special values: They provide acceleration, and they offer change of line without deceleration. Most racers can make at least a 20-degree line change without turning their skis; and they can accelerate while stepping. They leave tracks in the snow like those in Drawing 38 (next page).

The first turn in this sequence ends with a lateral step—allowing the skier to end his turn close to the fall line and still have a good line to approach the following gate. The second turn shows a classic skating step with forward thrust and direction change. This kind of turn provides muscle power acceleration only at slower racing speeds. The lateral step involves less change of leverage and body position than does the skating step. Thus it can be used in quicker gate situations.

(Drawing #38)

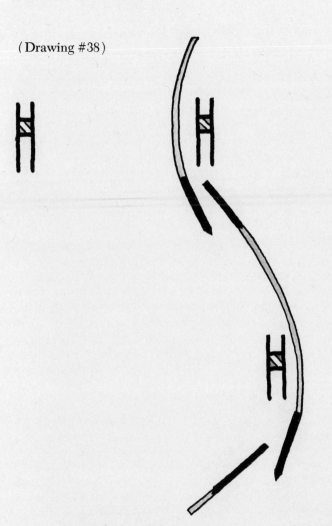

Attention must be given to use of your hands in skating turns. Whenever you have a solid platform from which to step, your hands and arms should move dynamically forward. The momentum they generate helps to carry your body forward and over the newly weighted ski. This hand action is similar to that used in making a standing broadjump or a racing dive. (See Photo 31.)

Good step turns require a solid platform (edge-locked ski) from which to push. Carved turns and edge lock traverses are a prerequisite to all stepping turns. Note the solid platform Russell is stepping from in Photo 31; also the platform used by Pete Murphy in Photo 32.

There are two basic kinds of skating turn:

1.   A dynamic skating step, where the inside ski is lifted clean off the snow and is placed down on another track, as in the pictures of Russel and Murphy, below.

2.   "Scissor turns," where the inside ski maintains snow contact while turning sharper than the outside ski. In this turn, common to many slalom and giant slalom maneuvers, the feet are steered independently. The uphill ski is turned more degrees than the downhill ski, and the racer ends the turn following the inside ski with his body weight. Joubert calls this "cramponage." Better control and a continuing feel for the snow are maintained by keeping the scissoring ski in the snow. Scissor turns are done when there is insufficient

31. Note the forward thrust of Patrick Russell's arms as he steps from his right to his left ski. This photo angle shows clearly the balance differential between the two skis. Russell's hip position is forward of his right foot, but behind his left. The time required to achieve a position of neutral leverage over the left ski may involve 6 to 15 feet of lineal distance in the course. When there is limited time to adjust leverage, a pure lateral step must be used so forward-aft balance is identical on right and left skis.

PHOTOPRESS

32.   MALCOLM REISS

time or too much speed for the major movements of a full skating step. (See Photo 33.)

For most skating turns, the skier pushes off the uphill edge of his downhill ski. and *steps onto the uphill edge of his uphill ski*. The turn back to the fall line is then initiated by rolling the uphill ski from uphill edge to downhill edge and applying turning power. Most lateral steps are also made from uphill edge to uphill edge; but it is occasionally useful to step to the downhill edge of the uphill ski. This movement is easiest when turning on relatively flat terrain, and close to the fall line. No edge change is then required to initiate the following turn.

Photos
31, 32

To effectively utilize step turns, you must be entirely comfortable on one foot—uphill or downhill. On all kinds of terrain you must move freely from one foot to the other. You must be comfortable traversing and turning on the uphill edge of your uphill ski. You must be in perfect balance and able to steer and carve turns on one foot. It is excellent practice to ski full-mountain runs on one ski. Practice at carving turns on one ski illustrates many facets of balance and edge control more effectively than two-ski maneuvers.

As step turns offer advantages in both acceleration and line, they should be used whenever time between gates permits, and reasonable balance can be maintained. Many short, quick turns require the full strength of both legs to execute. But most other turns are easily initiated or completed with stepping motions.

33. John Foster, from Steamboat Springs, Colorado, executes a scissor turn at the Junior Nationals. Note how well he is balanced on his inside ski. Hand and body positions are relaxed and natural. He makes this scissor turn with quiet efficiency.

MALCOLM REISS

Step turns should be taught at the very beginning of ski-school teaching sequences, and they should be stressed for young racers. They are not difficult maneuvers to be expected only from accomplished racers.

When free-skiing, especially at slow speeds, good racers initiate the majority of their turns with some degree of stepping motion. Beginning from a wide-track parallel stance, by simply picking up the inside ski, inward lean is achieved relative to the outside ski. A slight inward movement of the knee provides angulation, balance, and edge angle for the turn. When standing on one foot, pressure is doubled on the outside ski; this provides reverse camber. Every requirement of a turn is present but forward leverage and/or steering. A slight movement of the knee provides that. There is no easier way to turn snow skis than to move lightly from one foot to another in this way. Learn to do so with precision and grace.

As many skiers are not, by nature, good at skating motions, I recommend the following: On an open hill, run skating races—both uphill and down, or around in circles. The uphill races develop pushing power in the legs. The downhill races develop the coordination required for skating at high speeds. The circles teach every phase of balance and edge lock required for step turns. Learn to make strong forward arm movements with each step.

Photo 33

If you have opportunities to ice skate, take advantage of them. Use hockey or figure skates, as their rocked soles allow you to carve turns. Many aspects of balance, anticipation, and angulation are common to skating and skiing. If you are a week-end skier, mid-week skating is the best training you can do.

One of the best early season conditioning exercises that skiers can do is to run skating races on a football field. Just a few inches of snow provides adequate cover. Figure 8's around the goal posts make excellent training. It's seven laps to the mile! Sprint races from twenty to fifty yards are especially useful, as they require maximum thrust and quickness with each step.

Skiers who have mastered step turns use them at all speeds when they have time between gates and a stable platform to push from. Good downhillers make step turns at 70 miles per hour! It's a basic way to change edge and direction on snow skis.

chapter 26
Miscellaneous Tips

1. Stay in good physical shape. Snow skiing requires incredible strength—especially giant slalom and downhill, where high speeds create excessive G forces in many turns. If you are serious about being a good skier, you must accept the responsibility of physical training. Weight-lifting, circuit training, running, yoga, gymnastics—all must be a part of a thorough conditioning program. To reach the top in snow skiing, you must be one of the most perfectly conditioned athletes in the world.

2. Learn to attack! Skiing is competitive. Even giant slalom is becoming a "sprint." Never coast out of a starting gate, even in training. Whenever you run courses *attack*. That must become a habit and instinctive to your skiing. Note the elements of attack in nearly every photo in this book! Young champions like Pete Murphy and Leith Lende, and world champions like Augert and Russell consistently demonstrate a more dynamic, attacking style than other competitors at their respective levels. Importantly, they combine this attack with technical precision and discipline.

3. Don't be misled by the oft-repeated advice from coaches that "good racers ride a flat ski." That's nonsense. *You ride as flat a ski as possible without sideslipping in turns and traverses.* That often requires all the edge you can get—45 degrees plus. (See photos throughout this book.) Good racers use their edges dynamically. They also use them sensitively—applying just the right amount of edge without jamming. Many coaches tell racers, "get off your edges." This doesn't mean to use less edge. It means to stop skidding; to finish each turn earlier and get edge lock in each traverse.

4. Work to maintain constant ski contact with the snow, except in step turns and very short turns that require quick edge-set and rebound.

Whenever your skis leave the snow, it takes time to reestablish a precise feeling for the snow, and to achieve the exact amount of edge required. Good skiers flow down a course always in contact with the snow. Many efficiencies are thus gained. Remember—you can't steer a car when the wheels are off the ground. The same goes for snow skis.

5. One of Killy's great talents was changing edge for the next turn earlier in each traverse than his opponents. By changing edge earlier and approaching each gate on the edges to be used in the new turn, Killy could best prepare his balance and collect his power for maximum effort at a precise time. The edge change requires many body movements and new adjustments to feel the snow perfectly. Get those problems behind you before the maximum effort of each direction change is required.

6. Study your ski tracks, and those of others, whenever you are training. If a skier ahead of you on a practice course makes a particularly good turn, try to follow his track exactly. Learn to listen to the sounds other skiers make in the snow. You thus learn about their edge control, skidding, etc.

7. Master pole plant timing. Very few young racers have developed proper timing for their pole plant. This creates delays in starting turns, especially in slalom. The pole plant is an integral part of the rhythm of many turns. Particularly at slower speeds where unweighting is required. A properly timed pole plant triggers the unweighting motion that initiates a turn. To learn correct pole use requires hours of concentration on exercises particularly devoted to that problem. Ask your coach for help.

Remember that you can only turn as quickly as you can plant your pole. Hand action must be well disciplined to minimize arm movement. Do short hop turns on a steep slope to find out how weak your pole plants are. Then practice quick hop turns on easy slopes. Master your problems on easy terrain, then increase the difficulty of your exercises. A pole plant is unnecessary for most high-speed skiing, and for many giant slalom turns. Learn to ski fast without pole plants. Maintain quiet and balanced upper-body positions.

8. When learning new skills and techniques, practice frequently on easy slopes. Get the fundamentals under control. Develop the muscle patterns and timing you need; then try harder terrain. If you try to learn new skills on too difficult terrain, you can become discouraged and perform so poorly that you develop bad habits.

9. Remember, you're not Russell or Killy. Some techniques that are valid for these exceptional athletes make no sense at all for other racers. The average skier must develop a sound technique—must work for discipline and control and precision. Too many racers try to copy styles they are not physically suited for. Know your limitations and respect them. Billy Kidd did pretty well by concentrating on fundamentals.

10. Don't watch the professional racers too carefully. They ski mostly short, easy hills, and their courses are wide-open slaloms or tight giant slaloms. Both are suited to extremely aggresive techniques. While these techniques may win thirty-second dual slaloms on the pro circuit, they may not be suitable for the longer and more varied courses required by amateur competition. Master your fundamentals first; then become a hustler when easy courses allow.

11. Be a coach—always watching other skiers and thinking about technique. The more aware you are, the more easily you will absorb skills from watching other racers. Think about technique. Learn your physics. Do a school term paper on the physics of a snow-ski turn. Talk technique with your friends. When coaches suggest changes in your technique, always ask *Why*, and understand *Why*. Insist that your technique meet the goals of efficiency, economy of motion, good balance, minimum skidding, use of your ski's design capabilities.

12. Take care of your equipment—perfect care! Any failure in this effort handicaps you by a given number of seconds for every race.

13. Experiment with wedges and heel lifts until your natural stance is perfectly balanced. Again, a failure in this area is a guaranteed handicap.

14. When free-skiing, always work for speed. Choose a slow line and ski fast on it. Only thus can you learn every technique for gaining maximum performance from your skis. Ski fast whenever possible; and ski full-mountain runs without stopping.

15. Avoid static positions on your skis. You must be *quiet* on your skis, but never frozen. Brooks Dodge says you must be "either going up or coming down." Static positions induce skidding.

16. Wax simply. Use one brand, and master it. The challenge in waxing is to be consistently good, and never to miss completely. Don't gamble on exotic formulas for a big win. Be consistent. Wax properly for all training sessions.

17. Keep warm. Don't be ashamed to wear mittens or two pairs of long underwear. Cold muscles are easily injured and slow to react. If you have tried to write when your hands are cold, you know how stiff cold muscles can become. Cold legs are equally slow. Dress extra warmly on race days so you are warm and loose in the starting gate.

18. Remember that only two or three racers of a given age ever make the U.S. Ski Team. The odds are about 1000 to 1 against you. Don't put all your eggs in the skiing basket. Alpine racing is a great sport. Enjoy it at whatever levels you achieve. Don't set goals so high you don't enjoy each step you climb on the ladder.

Do work hard. The essence of competitive sport is the challenge to do your best. Realize your full potential; be a perfectionist. But have an objective view of your limitations.

19. Don't be a point chaser. The purpose of points is to fairly evaluate one racer against another. By various extended efforts some racers do get slightly better points than they deserve. My advice is to ski one race at a time; ski to win on one course at a time. When you are really good, your points will show it soon enough. I have never known a *really good* racer who didn't have good points.

20. When you have an opportunity to ski all day for extended periods of time, don't ski more than three of four hours. If you do, your muscles will become stale—and probably your attitude as well.

No athlete in swimming, track, tennis, football, or any other sport trains more than half a day except for intensive training camps of ten days or less.

Skiers who "take a winter off from school" just to ski must have something else to do. Independent studies, a part-time job, a hobby—something.

21. Try to play as many sports as possible. Don't limit yourself to skiing unless you have a really good chance to make the National Team, and you are at least sixteen years old. Every sport you pursue will add to your strength and coordination and mental flexibility. Soccer, tennis, squash, water-skiing, gymnastics, speed-skating, swimming, baseball, hockey, lacrosse, golf, track, football, basketball—all these sports have taught me things about body mechanics that have been useful in skiing. The more sports skills you acquire, the more natural your balance instincts become for a variety of body motions. Be a complete athlete, not just a skier. When you are sixteen to eighteen, and you can see your way clearly to a fair chance of making it to national levels in competition, then specialization makes sense.

There are many rewards of competition in national and international sports. I support any youngster who has goals this high. The rewards are worth many sacrifices. But be a good citizen and a well-rounded person at all levels of sport.

22.   Remember the public. They pay premium lift-ticket prices that support ski areas. Whenever you race, remember that you are a guest of the area and of all who ski there. Competitive skiing can only function as long as it has the support and good will of the skiing public. Treasure that support, and nurture it.

23.   When you finish serious racing, find time to coach some youngsters who are growing up in skiing. Good coaches are needed everywhere in America. Wonderful kids are involved in ski racing; they need good coaches to help them realize their dreams. Give something back to the sport that has given you so much.

part VII
Especially
for Coaches

chapter 27

Your Responsibilities Before Training

Every racer has innate attributes of strength, coordination, and balance. A coach must help each of his charges to realize the full potential of those attributes. After physical training, you have three responsibilities to meet before you begin on-snow coaching:

1. You must help each racer to acquire the best equipment his budget allows. This includes guidance in brands purchased, and in length of skis and poles. You must help racers to select skis well suited to their size, weight, and technique.

2. You must teach each racer to perfectly maintain his skis and to correctly adjust his bindings. You must inspire in each racer a sense of pride in the daily performance of those tasks. If at all possible, you must provide a complete ski worshop at your training area.

3. You must carefully evaluate each racer's need for wedges and heel lifts. These must be provided so each racer's natural stance is perfectly balanced. As the season progresses, remember that boots break down and wedge needs can change by as much as 2 or 3 degrees. As your racers become sensitive to the feel of their skis in the snow, they will know when their wedge needs change.

Less than 10 per cent of the racers competing in the United States today have received coaching help that meets these requirements. Even at the National Team level, there are skiers who need wedges and heel lifts. They have reached the National Team because they have sufficient athletic ability to make the necessary compensations and remain competitive. But they are giving away precious seconds in every race. If more attention had been given by the National Team coaches to balancing each racer's stance, the U.S. Ski Team would have produced a far stronger record over the past ten years. Had junior coaches across the country done this balancing work, many youngsters whose names the public has never heard might have become international champions.

Knowing what I now do about balance and economy of motion, I can look back over the past decade and recall numerous gifted athletes who could have made the National Team if only some coach had given them proper wedges. I'm embarrassed and sad that I lacked the knowledge to help them five or ten years ago. The knowledge now exists; and every coach bears a responsibility to share it with his racers.

This book is not the place to present a "how to" coaching manual. I can only emphasize the need for sound instruction in basic technique. Racers must be taught how their skis work in the snow, and how to carve turns. They must understand the importance of balance and economy of motion. They must learn to judge everything they do on skis by the laws of physics. Racers from the age of ten should read this book and Joubert's books and other helpful works as they appear in print. A spirited awareness of technique must be nurtured in all racing programs.

Whenever I train racers, I tell them: "You must all be coaches." Many youngsters develop a keen eye for the technical strengths and weaknesses of their peers. Their coaching analyses are helpful to me, and to each other. The more technically aware youngsters become, the more quickly they absorb skills by watching and following better racers. This should be a primary source of every racer's technical development.

Similarly, a primary source of every coach's development must be in watching good racers. In my ten years of coaching, I have learned more from my students than I have taught them. Listen carefully to those you coach; and observe them carefully too. They are your greatest source of continuing discovery.

chapter 28
Additional Comments on Photographs

Throughout this book I have confined my comments on each photograph to the specific ideas in the accompanying text. Many of the photos deserve study in greater detail. The following additional comments are offered for serious students of racing technique.

Photo 1 Becky's stance on her skis is excellent. She is in a strong, upright position so that her skeletal structure carries most of her weight; her back and shoulder muscles are relaxed. Note how lightly weighted Becky's right ski is. She is preparing to step into the next turn. I cannot emphasize too strongly the importance of stepping in modern race technique—and in recreational skiing as well.

I am unhappy with Becky's left arm. It is too high, and it is raised more than the coming pole plant requires. Becky's hands are not working in the perfect balance which precision race technique demands. This photo was taken early in the competitive season, before Becky had done sufficient work on hand discipline. Making the same turn in April, she would have carried her left hand considerably lower. Becky's right arm is good. It is relaxed. It is bent comfortably at the elbow, allowing for balance adjustment by either extension or contraction. Her right arm does *not* pull her head and inside arm into the hill. Note her comfortable distance from the pole.

Becky's left knee illustrates her need to be wedged slightly on her outside edges in a level stance. Like most girls, when she bends her knees they collapse to the inside, creating too much edge angle on the downhill ski for the amount of inward body lean produced.

Note how little snow is displaced by Becky's left ski, and how the snow flows parallel to the groove in her ski rather than being sprayed at right angles to her direction of travel.

[199]

Photos 2A, B, C, D   This is a nearly perfect high-speed turn. Note the complete lack of movement in Becky's upper body. Her hands, arms, shoulders, and head maintain the same position throughout the turn. Becky's high tuck position leaves her in balance directly over the middle of her skis and able to apply forward leverage as required to carve this turn.

Note in Photos 2C and 2D that she is *stepping* into the next turn. By moving her left ski laterally, she places her body in an instantly angulated position to begin carving the right turn with minimum upper-body movement. Her wide stance is comfortable, stable, and efficient.

Photos 2E, F   These photos deserve the most careful study. Riding the chairlift at Burke Mountain, ski tracks like these can be seen wherever the racers have been free skiing. To leave tracks like these in the snow should be the goal of racers and recreational skiers alike. Becky can ski Burke Mountain from top to bottom without ever skidding more than she does in these photos.

Photo 3   Note the effect of James's forward leverage—the right ski tip carving into the snow and establishing the groove the entire ski will follow. James's left hand and shoulder are too low—an error common to almost all developing racers in the United States. Even many skiers on the World Cup circuit drop their inside hand and shoulder to duck poles. Wedge needs—thick side inside—are a contributing factor to excessive inward lean with the upper body. James would be in a more stable position and able to get closer to the pole if he used more hip angulation for this turn (compare to Orcel in Photo 6).

Photo 4   Note Terry's distance from the pole—that is the distance of his outside ski. He has left sufficient room between his skis and the pole to allow for the required angulation without striking the pole. Angulation cannot be compromised. For every speed and radius of turn a given amount of angulation is required both to assure the purchase of the edge and to balance the skier so that he does not fall to the outside of the turn. In this photo, a flatter ski would skid because the edge simply would not hold. If Terry had less inward lean (bicycle lean angle) he would fall to the outside, or would have to flatten his skis and let them skid to the outside of the turn in order to maintain his balance. Racers must determine the exact amount of angulation and inward lean required for each turn and then choose a line approaching the pole that allows them to carve the turn without skidding.

Terry's hands are dynamically forward, as they must always be in slalom. His right hand is too high for optimum balance, but this is probably required for the approaching pole plant. The desire for perfectly balanced hand positions is more often compromised in slalom than in giant slalom. The slalom skier is more concerned with getting close to each pole. More radical movements to get the inside hand and shoulder by the pole can be accepted at slalom speeds than at giant slalom speeds. Note that Terry's inside hand (left) is thrust forward, rather than down. This motion leads his shoulder by the pole at the same time as it provides momentum for the step he will take into the next turn.

Photo 5A   Cathy's hands are too low and her arms too stiff. She exhibits here the same errors that are common to her high-speed skiing. Basic faults in each skier's racing stance are almost always evident in slow-speed maneuvers. Despite Cathy's bulky parka, the tension in her shoulder muscles is evident in this photo. At this point, her coach should insist that she carry her hands and arms correctly—so it will become natural for her to do so at all times when she is skiing. Cathy is also sloppy about dragging her poles. Racers must strive for perfection in all aspects of their skiing; only thus can the best muscle habits be formed.

Photo 6   The line joining Orcel's hands forms a perfect right angle to his upper spine (waist to neck). This is a basic requirement for balanced hand positions. How many photos in this book illustrate this optimum hand balance? Orcel's hands are unusually wide here because they are providing balance for an especially dynamic turn.

Orcel's weight is almost entirely on his right ski. His high hip position and erect upper body provide optimum strength to resist the extreme centrifugal forces generated by this high-speed turn. A racer in a lower hip position, and more bent at the waist, simply would not have the strength to resist skidding in this turn.

Note that Orcel's head tilts just slightly toward his outside shoulder. Compare this to Photos 3, 4, 9, and 10; check this head position on all action photos in this book. If a skier's stance is correct and his upper body is relaxed, his head will naturally fall toward the outside shoulder because of its extreme weight. Because the head is heavy and is on the end of the fulcrum arm which your body is to your skis, any incorrect positioning of your head causes serious balance problems. Racers who drop their inside hand and shoulder often cause their head to lean inside a turn. This is a serious displacement of weight. Good racers do not think consciously about their head position; if other factors of stance are correct, the head balances correctly without conscious effort.

Photos 7A, B   Compare these photos to 29B and 30. The girls photographed are the same. In the latter pair of photos, it is Sarah who turns her hip and Leith who uses a more square hip position. Thus both girls illustrate their flexibility to react differently in each turn. Neither has a set technique. Each turn is a response to terrain, line, snow conditions, etc.

In 7A, Leith has completed more of the required direction change than Sarah has in 7B. This partly explains the difference in leverage apparent on each girl's left ski. Leith is ending her direction change, and so has moved to the middle and back of her ski. Sarah, still tightening the radius of her turn, has more pressure on the tip of her skis. In Photo 30, Leith exhibits her ability to use strong forward leverage to carve a turn.

In the slalom turns (29B and 30), Sarah exhibits superior hand discipline, but Leith is typically more aggressive. To combine aggressiveness with discipline and perfect balance is a primary challenge for every racer. Patrick Russell and Barbara Cochran best exemplify the combination of these factors.

In Photo 7A, Sarah's left arm is too straight. She has undoubtedly straightened it as a balance requirement demanded by some terrain difficulty encountered just before this picture was taken. This stiff left arm is not Sarah's "home position" or natural stance.

Special attention should be given to the extreme edge angle and angulation used by Leith and Sarah in the giant slalom turn. This photo of Sarah was selected for the cover of this book because it so clearly emphasizes edge angle, angulation, forward leverage, and the carving action of her ski in the snow.

Photo 9   Note the similarity between Billy Shaw's right arm here and Leith Lende's right arm in 7A. In both photos the arm is relaxed, is comfortably bent, and is effectively turned away from the pole. Both Leith and Billy have used a subtle arm motion here that does little to disturb their balance over their skis. I would prefer their inside hand to be a little higher, but neither racer allows the inside hand to draw the attached shoulder too low. Shaw keeps his shoulders especially level, and his head is tilting naturally to the outside. Leith's head in 7A appears to be leaning toward the pole—but I think she is beginning to move toward the next turn, stepping laterally to her right ski. She is using her head to lead the lateral projection of her upper body. This is a natural and unselfconscious motion.

Photos 13A, B   These photos perfectly illustrate Russell's ability to combine disciplined technique with extreme aggressiveness. Many American coaches and racers believe that racing technique is a "natural" thing, and that National Team skiers and other talented racers need very little technical coaching. "Go Fast" is their motto, and they believe that each racer will develop those natural techniques that are best suited for him. This belief is a serious handicap which the American ski team has long suffered with.

Skiing is a highly technical sport—like gymnastics, figure skating, and ballet. Attention must be given to the minutest details of technique if one expects to win in international competition. The very best American coaches have only a limited understanding of body mechanics, physics, ski design, etc. There is a pound of superstition for every ounce of knowledge in ski coaching today. We have long hours of research and reasoning to do. Our best skiers do not yet have coaching equivalent to that available to skaters, swimmers, and dancers.

There is no member of the U.S. Men's Ski Team who, if photographed in the same place as Russell in turns 13A and 13B, would exhibit an equally well-balanced and disciplined stance on his skis. That is the simple and painful truth which American coaches and racers must humbly accept. America's most successful racers—the Cochrans—have succeeded because their father is a technician of world-class caliber, and he has more perfectly trained his children than other Americans have been trained.

To succeed in international racing, we must become as technically precise and disciplined as ballet dancers: they train 6 to 8 hours per day for 10 to 15 years before they become acknowledged masters of their dancing art. And their floor is always level! Skiers who would be champions in the next decade must combine superb conditioning with a much greater technical discipline than has yet been recognized as necessary in the sport of skiing.

In Photo 13A, Russell is in a lower hip position than would be comfortable for most racers. He has strength and balance sufficient to maintain complete control at this point on the course. This photo was taken at the *end* of Russell's turn—at the point at which he achieves edge-lock and lets his skis run toward the next gate. Russell seldom begins turns in this position. Russell is using subtle back leverage to end a turn requiring little direction change where the terrain is not difficult. Compare this picture to that of Orcel in Photo 6. If Russell were approaching the same gate as Orcel, he would almost certainly be in an upright stance offering maximum strength, agility, and use of forward leverage.

Photo 13B deserves careful study with an awareness of the agility which Russell's stance provides. He is erect, square, balanced. He can move with lightning speed in any direction. Compare Russell's hand position here to Leslie Orton's hands in 13D. Can you see that Leslie's body is restricted by the imbalance of her hands? To appreciate this, stand on a level floor and hold your hands as Russell does, and see how quickly you can move both feet in any direction. Then copy Leslie's hand position and try to make the same quick movements. You will feel your lowered arm constrict muscles in that whole side of your body; this reduces your agility by a significant amount. You must perform these exercises to fully appreciate my comments. Or talk with a world class-ballet dancer. He will tell you that a hand or arm just one inch from the optimum position will prohibit the perfect execution of a given movement. Figure skaters are equally aware. Skiers, because their sport is so dynamic and their platform so much more varied than the ice arena or dance floor, have failed to appreciate the finest details of body mechanics.

Photos 13C, D   Compare Augert's hands (and also Russell's in 13A, B) to Leslie Orton's hands. Leslie's inside hand, like that of most American racers, is too low. She is not in *perfect* balance. Her inside arm draws just a little more of her weight to the inside ski than is desirable in this turn. Her position is good enough to win the American Junior Nationals, but not good enough to win in international competition.

Photo 14   This use of extreme forward leverage by Augert ought no more to be copied for most ski turns than Russell's squatting position in 13A. A comparison of these pictures emphasizes the great versatility of modern skis—the range of movements to which the skis respond. In both cases the ski is controlled by edge angle, pressure, and leverage. Each skier's body position determines the range of movements possible to him in the next few hundredths of a second.

Are Augert's arms too straight? Is he bent too much at the waist? Is he carrying too much weight on his inside ski? This turn is so dynamic it is difficult to pass judgement. Augert is reacting to strong forces of momentum. A study of the snow patterns under his skis indicates that as much as 70 percent of Augert's weight is on his left (inside) ski. Would a picture taken six feet earlier show Augert's arms comfortably bent? Has he extended them to effectively alter his balance and lead his body back over the outside ski? That is possible —and it would be a proper use of the hands. They are "balance adjusters."

It is also possible that Augert is intentionally weighting his left ski —that he is completing a scissors turn and is moving to make his left ski the outside ski in the following turn. If this is the case, then he is using his arms to lead his body across his left ski and eventually inside the ski for a right turn. He must somehow get from a left lean to a right lean as he changes edge and direction. I think this latter case is the more probable. Note the direction in which Augert is looking— presumably toward the next gate.

Photos 16A, B   Both Pete and Chris exhibit the error of carrying their inside hand too low. Every other aspect of their stance and technique is world-class. This failure in hand discipline may not hurt them in this turn, but it reduces their margin for balance error, and it may cause them problems in a more difficult turn.

Photo 17   Study this picture carefully. Consider what happens to my left ski if I move my knee two inches forward or back. What will happen if the ski is edged five degrees more or less. How would I change the edge angle? It is easier to visualize these effects in a photo of a slow-speed maneuver, just as it is easier to experiment with various inputs to the ski while doing slow maneuvers. As figure skaters master their craft doing school figures, so racers should develop a full understanding of technique doing slow turns. Note my erect and balanced stance.

Photos 18 and 19   The track of my inside ski shows no skid resistance at all. Look at Photo 19 and you will see that Mary Beth leaves an identical track with her inside ski. I have never discussed this inside ski track with my racers. Mary Beth did this instinctively—because she has learned to eliminate skidding from her ski technique whenever possible. Her natural feel for the *glissement* of her skis caused her to balance lightly on the inside ski as the track shows. Note the reverse camber in Mary Beth's left ski.

Photo 24   This photo, as well as all the action pictures in this book, should convince people that the best racers do not "ride a flat ski." Had Augert aimed the tip of his skis at the pole in this turn, consider how far he would have had to skid his skis to pass the pole as he does.

Photo 25   Note the reverse camber of Biechu's skis. His stance in this photo is extremely well balanced and effective.

Photo 26   Notice how close together Serrat's feet are. This narrow stance detracts from his balance and agility. Though "feet together parallel skiing" has long been the goal of most recreational skiers, it is clearly an inefficient style that hampers free and balanced movement on skis. All skiers—recreational and racer alike—must learn to use their feet independently and not to be confined by too narrow a stance.

Photos 29A and 30   In 29A Lyndall appears slightly too bent at the waist. This reduces her agility and the quickness with which she can step into the next turn. Her left hand is carried too wide. Consider the lateral movement Lyndall must make with her left hand to clear the next pole. How will this movement affect pressure, leverage, and edge angle on Lyndall's skis? By contrast, Leith's left arm is in perfect position for the next pole. Leith should not drop her right arm so low. Leith too often lowers her inside arm as she passes a pole. Consider the unnecessary time, change of pressure on the skis, and effect on back and shoulder muscles which this arm movement requires.

Conclusion: Although I have spoken mainly of body positions in these appended comments, please note that I have not discussed body positions as inputs to rotational turning force. Rather, the discussion has been related to efficiency and balance. Hand and arm positions are important less for what they do than for what they prohibit you from doing. Improper upper–body positions detract from what a racer can do with his lower body and skis to create turns.

Nearly all of the photos discussed here are of racers who carve turns by use of the basic concepts outlined in this book. The mastery of efficient body positions makes it possible for one racer to beat another by being in continually better balance and having more precise control of edge angle, pressure, and leverage on his skis.

East Burke, Vermont
July, 1972